financial planning and monitoring

WITHDRAWN

David Cox, FCCA FCIB Cert Ed
Michael Fardon, BA MPhil ACIB Cert Ed

Osborne Books *GNVQ* Series

acknowledgements

The authors would like to thank the following people who have helped in the preparation of this book: Paula Clarke, Jean Cox, Alan Hardwick, Cajiten D'Silva and Martyn Roads of BTEC. The authors are particularly grateful to Roger Petheram for his continued support and advice during the writing of the book.

The authors also thank BTEC and J Sainsbury plc for permission to reproduce published material.

authors

David Cox is a freelance lecturer and writer. Until recently he was a Senior Lecturer in the Management and Professional Studies Department at Worcester College of Technology. He is a Fellow of The Chartered Association of Certified Accountants. He has over twenty years' full-time teaching experience, during which he has taught accounting students at all levels. He is the author or joint author of a number of textbooks, including *Business Accounts, Accounting, Business Record Keeping, Finance* and *Financial Recording* from Osborne Books.

Michael Fardon has followed a career in domestic and international banking, in teaching, writing and publishing. He lectured for a number of years in finance and accounting at Worcester College of Technology. He is joint author of a number of textbooks, including *Accounting, Business Record Keeping, Finance* and *Financial Recording* from Osborne Books. He is currently developing teaching material for GNVQ Business courses, and is a co-author and editor of Osborne Books' *Business Studies*, written for GNVQ Advanced Level, *Introduction for Business* for GNVQ Intermediate Level and *Foundation Business* for GNVQ Foundation Level.

copyright

Published by Osborne Books Limited,
Gwernant, The Common, Lower Broadheath, Worcester, WR2 6RP, Tel 0905 333691

Printed by the Bath Press, Avon.

British Library Cataloguing in Publication Data
A catalogue record for this book is available from the British Library

ISBN 1-872962-75-0

contents

introduction

This book has been written specifically for the BTEC *Financial Planning and Monitoring* option unit for GNVQ Advanced Level. It covers precisely the performance criteria and range statements set down by BTEC. The BTEC Rationale for the unit is:

> *"The purpose of the unit is to examine the way in which organisations use financial information in order to make business decisions and evaluate their effect. This can be seen as a continuous cycle involving the setting of objectives, the measurement of activities and comparison of actual and planned outcomes. The feedback is then used to modify future plans as appropriate and the cycle continues."*

The book is divided into four sections which correspond with the four unit elements:

1   Financial planning and management (BTEC Element 11.1)

2   Budgeting (BTEC Element 11.2)

3   Monitoring costs (BTEC Element 11.3)

4   Decision making (BTEC Element 11.4)

It is assumed that students taking this option unit will be familiar already with the 'nuts and bolts' of basic accounting from their coverage of the financial mandatory units. It is also assumed that they will be familiar with the outline of a business plan. In this book these concepts are taken a stage further and the planning and monitoring processes used in business examined in greater depth.

The *Financial Planning and Monitoring* unit involves not only an appreciation of business planning techniques, but also the development of practical numerical and information technology skills: for example the preparation of budgets using computer spreadsheets. To help students to develop these skills, the authors have included comprehensive student activities at the end of each chapter.

Assessment of the *Financial Planning and Monitoring* unit should involve students investigating real businesses. To help in this process four Evidence Collection Exercises – one for each element – are included in the text. It would be useful if the school or college could make contact with a number of local business organisations in order to obtain information, arrange visits and talks to help with these projects. This should enable students to gain a wider appreciation of current business practice.

David Cox
Michael Fardon

Summer 1994

Section

1

financial planning
and management

1 Business planning

introduction

Business planning in very simple terms means 'getting your business to where you want it to go'. Monitoring in equally simple terms is 'making sure it gets there' by constantly reviewing progress. Behind these simplifications lies a complex process which forms the subject matter for the whole of this book.

You will note that the title of the book is 'financial' planning and monitoring. Many aspects of business are measured in money terms: sales figures, profit figures, the cost of labour and materials, for example. Business planning therefore to a large extent involves a 'financial' view of the organisation. Business targets and success rates, as we will see, are often measured in money terms.

In this chapter we take an overview of business planning and monitoring and examine the way a business plans for the future by

- setting its objectives – for example, to achieve a target rate of profitability, to capture a stated percentage of the market for its product
- gathering information – much of it financial – which will enable it to see where it stands at present in terms of its products, its sales and profits
- adopting plans which will enable the business to get where it wants, eg the expansion of its operations, the introduction of new products and services
- monitoring the situation as time goes on so that the success of the plans can be assessed and corrective action taken if necessary

In this chapter we will see that the planning process for the larger business – a public limited company involves for example:

- long-term strategic 'corporate' plans – the setting of broad objectives
- short-term 'operational' plans – involving plans and budgets for different areas of the business, eg sales, production, staffing

The planning process requires information, and we will examine the type of information gathered internally and externally by the business. We will also look at how the business assesses and evaluates the information – seeing whether it is useful, reliable and up-to-date.

the business planning process

the business plan and business planning

In this book we will be examining the internal planning process of a business in detail. It is important not to confuse this with the 'business plan' document you will probably have already encountered in your studies (see Osborne Books *Business Studies,* Chapter 47).

The 'business plan' is a formal written document compiled normally when a business wants to raise finance. It is presented to the prospective lender and sets out in a persuasive way why lending to the business (or investing in the business) is a feasible proposition. The business plan is the way a business 'sells itself' to a provider of finance, such as a bank.

The important point about a business plan is that it is not *the* one and only plan prepared by the organisation: it is the result of internal planning processes involving many different plans – sales, production, staffing, for example. It can be seen as the end product of the internal planning processes which we will be examining in this book.

business planning and business size

In this book we will be examining in detail the planning processes that take place in larger businesses, a public limited company for example. The reason for this is that, in a larger organisation, the planning process is of necessity more developed and formalised. This is not to say that smaller businesses, a sole trader, for example, do not use the same planning principles. *All* businesses, when approaching a lender, will need to compile the business plan document referred to above. The planning principles remain the same, whatever the size of the business.

the planning and monitoring cycle

Businesses – and individuals too – are constantly planning ahead. The individual may be planning to buy a car or go on holiday; the business may be planning a specific project, or it may be looking at the year ahead in order to calculate staffing and estimate sales. Whatever the situation, there are normally *four distinct stages* in the planning process:

1. *set objectives* – for example, a business may aim to increase sales by 25%
2. *look at the situation using financial information* – can the business produce 25% more goods? how much will it cost? where can it sell 25% more goods?
3. *make a specific plan* – the business can expand production, take on more staff, start exporting goods to Europe
4. *see how the business is getting on* – the business can look at its sales figures each month, see if it is achieving its target, and do something about it if it is not

Now study the planning and monitoring diagram in fig. 1.1 on the next page.

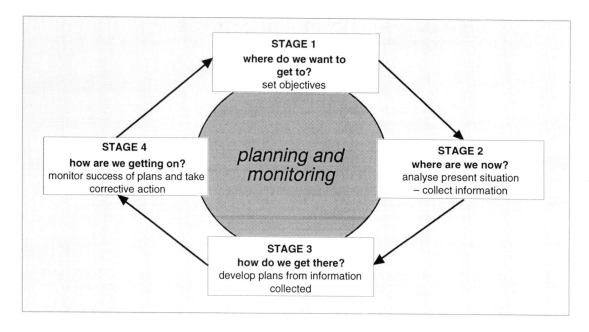

Fig 1.1 The planning and monitoring cycle

You will see from the diagram that the four stages of the planning process are presented in the form of a *cycle*. The monitoring stage ("how are we getting on?") leads directly back to the first stage again ("where do we want to get to?"). This is common to all planning processes: once you have set your objectives and put them into action, you will be reviewing progress and seeing where you can get to next. On a personal level, someone planning a holiday may decide to go to Spain, and then will get food poisoning on the second day of the holiday. The monitoring stage – "how are we getting on?" has a very definite answer: "I will never go there again, it's going to be Blackpool next year." Taking the example on the previous page, the business expanding sales by 25% may find that it has a runaway success in selling to Europe, and may decide to step up production and increase sales by a further 25% the following year. In both cases, the planning process is seen to be *continuous*, as fig 1.1 illustrates.

In the remainder of this chapter we will look in detail at each of the four stages of the planning cycle.

stage one: setting objectives

objectives

If you refer back to the introduction to this chapter (page 4), you will recall that businesses need to know where they are going and how they are going to get there. This is the essence of the planning process. There is a clear distinction between:

* setting objectives

* making plans to put the objectives into action

Setting objectives is a process which can be expressed in two forms: the *mission statement* and the *corporate objectives*.

Note that we will illustrate this process by reference to a public limited company business (plc): the term 'corporate' means 'relating to companies'. This is not to say that smaller businesses or public sector organisations do not write mission statements or formulate objectives; in fact it is very important that they do so.

mission statement

A mission statement should set out simply and as succinctly as possible:

- what the business does
- what it aims to achieve
- the values and standards it will adopt

Let us take a new producer of Italian pasta dishes as an example. Its mission statement might read:

"Bella Foods plc is a specialist food manufacturer which aims to supply fresh ready-made quality pasta dishes to the major food retailers in the European Union."

setting objectives

While the mission statement is intended as a general explanation of what the business does and how it does it, *objectives* are specific statements, intended to give the business and its workforce a sense of purpose and direction. They often cover:

- *profitability*
  Profitability is often measured as 'Return on Capital Employed', ie the relationship between net profit and capital expressed as a percentage:

$$\frac{\text{net profit for the year } \times \ 100}{\text{capital employed at the start of the year}} \quad = \quad \text{Return on Capital Employed}$$

  If you are unsure about these terms, refer to Osborne Books' *Business Studies,* Chapter 39. In simple terms, Return on Capital Employed measures the amount of profit a business will produce in relation to the amount of money invested by its owners (eg shareholders). An example of a profitability objective might be:

  "Bella Foods aims to achieve an annual Return on Capital Employed of 15%."

- *market share*
  A target will often be set for the market share the business plans to capture within a certain time period, for example:

  "Bella Foods plans to account for 20% of European Union sales of fresh pasta dishes within three years."

- **product range**

  The objectives may include a statement setting out the policy for expanding the range of products offered by the business, for example:

  "Bella Foods will bring out one new pasta dish every two months over the next three years."

- **environmental policy**

  The business will often state its environmental and 'green' policy as a specific objective, for example:

  "Bella Foods will not use additives or artificial colourings in its products, and will use biodegradeable packaging wherever possible."

- **Human Resources policy**

  The business will achieve its objectives better if it has a well-trained and motivated workforce. Its objectives may include a statement such as:

  "Bella Foods will provide a structured programme ofcomprehensive training for its skilled workforce, and provide a wide range of staff benefits."

Clearly the process of setting objectives and writing mission statements are closely allied (see fig. 1.2 below). See also fig. 1.3 on page 10 for an example of corporate objectives from J Sainsbury plc.

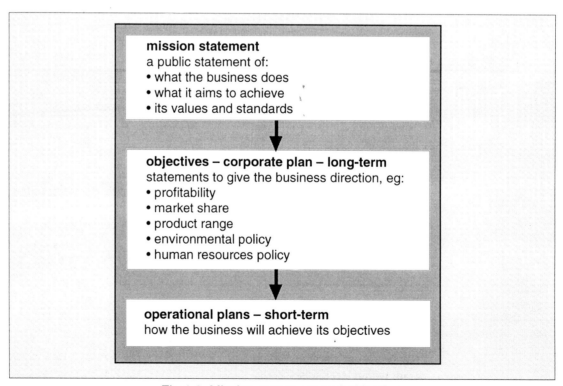

mission statement
a public statement of:
• what the business does
• what it aims to achieve
• its values and standards

objectives – corporate plan – long-term
statements to give the business direction, eg:
• profitability
• market share
• product range
• environmental policy
• human resources policy

operational plans – short-term
how the business will achieve its objectives

Fig 1.2 Mission statement and objectives

objectives and plans

In stage 3 of the planning cycle, objectives are turned into plans. We will deal with the planning process in detail later in the chapter, but it is useful to note now that there are two specific types of plan, the first of which directly involves objectives:

the 'Corporate Plan'

Objectives, such as those quoted on the previous pages, are used to compile the *Corporate Plan*. It is important to note that a Corporate Plan should involve all aspects of business activities: it is a *co-ordinated approach*, and not just a list of things to achieve. The timescales of the Corporate Plan are generally long-term (up to, say, seven years) and will vary from business to business. A car manufacturer will work with long timescales, eg seven years, because cars take a long time to develop from design stage to production. On the other hand, a fashion clothes manufacturer which operates in a volatile market will only be able to plan ahead for a much shorter period of time.

Corporate Plans will involve the directors and senior management of a business, and are said to be 'strategic' in nature – they deal with large issues.

operational plans

The Corporate Plan defines where a business is going in the long term. Operational plans set out how the objectives will be achieved a year at a time. Operational plans involve the middle and lower levels of management, and are said to be 'tactical' in nature – they deal with day-to-day decisions.

conflicting objectives

Do not assume that the directors and managers of a business will just happily settle down one day around a table and write a series of objectives. There are a number of underlying *conflicts* in formulating objectives. For example, the Finance Director of a company may insist on maximum profitability. He or she has the interests of the shareholders in mind and also the need for the company to survive in a competitive environment. How will he deal with the following demands on the company's cash?

- the Production Director wants to channel more funds into product development; he says the company cannot advance its product range without more money being invested in research and more modern production facilities

- the Sales Director wants higher commission rates for the sales representatives; he says that he is losing staff to competitors who offer better rates of pay

- the Managing Director says she is concerned about environmental policy; she suggests packaging made from more expensive recycled material

There is no set 'answer' to these problems. The business will inevitably have to compromise and resolve the conflict between the objectives, while making sure that no single objective is completely sacrificed. You will no doubt be able to think of examples of businesses where certain objectives become secondary to profitability and efficiency, particularly in the public sector.

Company Objectives

To discharge the responsibility as leaders in our trade by acting with complete integrity, by carrying out our work to the highest standards, and by contributing to the public good and to the quality of life in the community.

To provide unrivalled value to our customers in the quality of the goods we sell, in the competitiveness of our prices and in the range of choice we offer.

In our stores, to achieve the highest standards of cleanliness and hygiene, efficiency of operation, convenience and customer service, and thereby create as attractive and friendly a shopping environment as possible.

To offer our staff outstanding opportunities in terms of personal career development and in remuneration relative to other companies in the same market, practising always a concern for the welfare of every individual.

To generate sufficient profit to finance continual improvement and growth of the business whilst providing our shareholders with an excellent return on their investment.

Fig 1.3 Company objectives of J Sainsbury plc

stage two: collecting information

the need for information

Any planning process requires you to look at your present situation before making plans for the future. If you are buying a car you will want to know how much money you have, how much money a car costs, and what cars are on the market. Your choice of a Lada or a Porsche will depend very much on these factors. You may even decide that you cannot afford a car yet, or you may not be old enough for the licence, or you may live in the middle of a large city where a car may not necessarily be an advantage.

The same planning choices face a business: – should it buy a new computer? – does it need more staff? – should it increase the range of products it sells? It is very clear that the need for accurate and reliable information, much of it financial in nature, is essential for the making of planning decisions.

what type of information?

Information may be classified in a number of ways:

*   *past information* – evidence of what has happened in the past
*   *current information* – the present situation
*   *future information* – forecasts

In addition, information may come from two different types of source; it may be:

*   *internal information* – from within the business
*   *external information* – from outside sources

We will now illustrate these classifications of information by reference to a manufacturing company. When you read through the text, you should be able to relate the categories of information to other types of business as well.

past information

internal sources	external sources
market share last year	competitors' market share last year
last year's sales	competitors' sales for last year
last year's profits	competitors' profits for last year
advertising costs	competitors' advertising costs
stock levels	competitors' stock levels
rates of pay	competitors' rates of pay

As you will see, much of the information is *financial* in nature or by implication. Sales, profits and costs (eg advertising) are clearly expressed in money terms. Stock levels are expressed either in items, or in money values. The implications of stock holding are financial – stock has to be bought and warehousing has to be paid for. Rates of pay will dictate the wages bill of a business, often a very significant cost.

current information

internal sources	external sources
size and value of premises	competitors' premises
number of employees	competitors' employees
machine capacity	competitors' facilities
delivery times	competitors' delivery times
quality of goods	competitors' quality ratings
contracts in hand	competitors' contracts

future information

Note that the information here relates less to competitors and more to general external conditions:

internal sources	external sources
investment plans	raw material prices
proposed new products	foreign currency exchange rates
expansion into new markets	economic forecasts
requirements for new staff	likely political changes

sources of information

Information may be gathered from a number of sources:

internal information

Internal information may be obtained from:

- the *financial statements* of the business – the profit and loss account, balance sheet and cashflow statement
- the *fixed asset register* – a list containing details (including a valuation) of fixed assets (eg premises, equipment) owned by the business
- *management reports*, for example from Sales Department, setting out the breakdown of sales figures:
  - the amount of sales for each product
  - the amount of sales for each geographic area
  - the money amount of sales made to each customer
- other management reports including stock values, production levels, payroll

external information

External information includes:

- competitors financial statements (limited companies' reports are publicly available from Companies House)
- other financial information about competitors which may be unofficially available, (note that industrial espionage is not normally acceptable practice!)

- competitors' catalogues and price lists
- official statistics – employment statistics, reports on industry profit margins
- trade journals
- market research reports
- the financial press

analysis of information

The information gathered will enable the business to assess its current position, and enable it to judge how successful it is in comparison with its competitors. Areas it will assess (and the appropriate sources of information) will be:

- its profitability – from the profit and loss account
- its ability to invest in future expansion – from its balance sheet
- its sales performance – from the profit and loss account and management reports
- its efficiency in terms of production – from management reports
- its labour costs – from the profit and loss account and management reports

When analysing information it will look for:

trends

External sources of information will enable the business to plan its products and future production plans in line with trends in markets for its goods, the price of raw materials, shifts in employment patterns and in the import and export situation. For example:

- phasing out products which are in the declining stage of their life cycle – eg unfashionable clothes
- a change in the materials from which a product is made if the price of raw materials rises – eg furniture made of laminated chipboard rather than solid wood
- use of part-time employees and job-sharing schemes, made possible by higher levels of unemployment
- stopping UK production of goods which can be imported cheaply – eg mass market hi-fi and cameras which are more expensive to produce in the UK

major changes in the market

Businesses will need to plan carefully to deal with major changes in the market such as competitors' price changes (as in the case of 'storewars' – the food supermarkets' price cutting), and technological changes (eg CDs superseding black vinyl records).

limitations of information

A business should be aware of the limitations of information gathered. It should always test information by certain benchmarks. Information should always be:

- accurate
- up-to-date
- relevant
- reliable

Dangers of information gathering include:

- inaccurate forecasts – a problem with external information

- biased information – a problem with internal information, eg an over-enthusiastic sales representative exaggerating potential sales of a new product

- unreliable external information – it is always good practice to look for confirmation of external data by using several sources

stage three: developing plans

operational plans

The *operational* planning process follows the setting of objectives (ie the Corporate Plan) and the gathering of internal and external information. The business will need to know where it stands in terms of:

- its products and markets

- the direction in which the industry is going (ie expanding or declining)

- its financial position and profitability

- external influences – the economy and the political situation

The business can then set in motion one year operational plans in all areas. These will set specific targets for the business. Study the diagram set out below in fig 1.4, and then read the text on the next page.

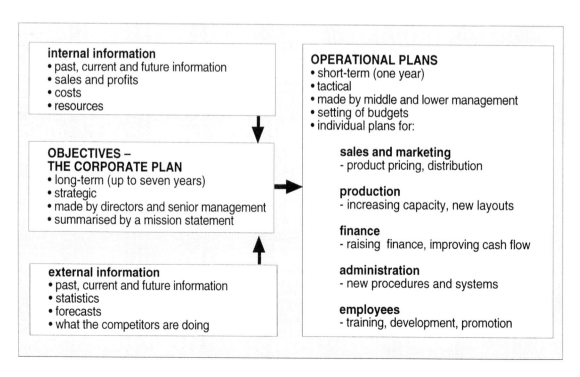

Fig 1.4 Operational planning

As you will see from fig 1.4, operational plans have a number of features:

departmental and functional plans

Operational plans are normally set by individual *departments* within the business – eg sales and marketing, production, finance – and will be the responsibility of the departmental manager. In the next chapter we will examine the structure of a business and look at the decision-making process at different levels within the business.

Operational plans set out the detail dictated by the objectives of the business, eg the number of products produced, pay rates, the amount of finance to be raised, the introduction of new technology. Some plans are set by *function*, eg staffing, and will cover a single function within all departments of a business. The examples of plans (and their contents) shown in fig. 1.4 are typical of a large manufacturing company: the actual number and type of plans will vary from organisation to organisation.

short-term plans

Operational plans are normally set for one financial year at a time. Plans are constantly reviewed and monitored by the people responsible for them. Towards the end of each year, new plans will be drawn up for the following year, taking into account all the developments during the current year. Operational plans must always keep in mind the requirements of the long-term Corporate Plan – the objectives of the business.

tactical decisions

Whereas the Corporate Plan involves long-term *strategic* decisions made by directors and senior management, operational plans involve day-to-day *tactical* decisions made by middle and lower management. Strategic planning in business might involve building a new factory in the West Midlands, operational planning will deal, for example, with the day-to-day decisions of how to set out the production line, how much to pay the workers, and how to distribute the manufactured goods.

budget setting

Operational plans involve the setting of budgets by departments and also by function. Budgets are explained in detail in Chapter 3, but it is important when examining the planning process to define budgets and set them in context.

A budget is a means of planning and control used by the management of a business to achieve stated objectives

A budget is based on information – past and current – and forecasts. It covers a set period of time, normally a year. A budget can deal with:

* *income* – eg from sales
* *expenditure* – eg production: cost of materials, cost of labour

You will know on a personal level that a household budget estimates the amount of money it costs to run the household in terms of mortage repayments, fuel bills, food, travel and entertainment based on a set income. A business budget formalises this process: it looks at projected income or expenditure over the year under various categories ('budget heads'), and monitors the situation regularly (often every four weeks).

Budgets are set by individual departments, and are linked closely to performance targets for those departments. The departmental managers – the *budget holders* – become responsible for spending up to their budget limit and meeting targets. The production department, for example, must meet production targets but also keep spending within defined limits. Such a department is known as a *cost centre*.

Budgets are also useful for functions within a business; a staffing budget (which covers all departments) will tell a business how much it will cost to pay its employees at a given rate of pay. If this rate of pay changes, the staffing budget will tell the management what the new wages bill will be.

stage four: monitoring plans

the monitoring process

The operational plans for each department or function will need monitoring carefully so that if any problem arises it can be dealt with. The monitoring process can be both:

- *large scale* – part of the review of the activity of the business as a whole, ie 'how is the business getting on?'

- *detailed* – part of the departmental budgeting process, ie 'how well is the Sales and Marketing Department achieving its targets this month?'

Fig. 1.5 below illustrates the overall (large scale) monitoring of business success.

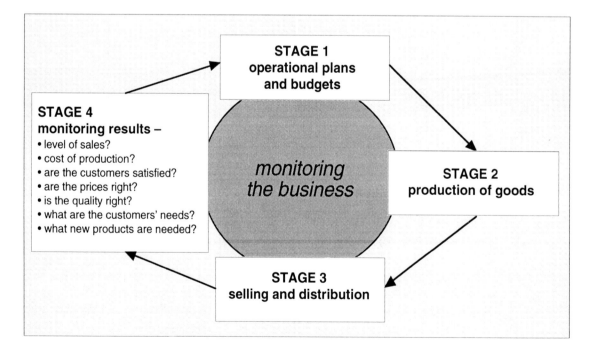

Fig 1.5 Overall monitoring of the business

Fig 1.5 on the previous page shows that the monitoring process of a business is a continuous cycle. Operational plans are made for a twelve month period in line with the general objectives of the business, the goods are produced and sold (or a service may be provided) and then the business looks for feedback from the customers so that it can judge how successful the product has been. This feedback can be found from internal and external sources:

- *the actual sales figures:*
    – what is the level of sales for each product?
    – have the targets in the sales budget been reached?
- *after-sales service:*
    – how many items have been returned?
    – what complaints have been received?
- *pricing:*
    – how do the prices compare with those of the competitors?
- *questionnaires* circulated to customers providing feedback about:
    – customer satisfaction
    – the quality of the product
- *market research:*
    – carried out by the business itself
    – carried out by specialist agencies

This feedback will enable the business to judge what customer *needs* are, and to plan ahead and budget for the following year. The business may need to modify existing products, or it may need to introduce new ones. So the process continues.

budget monitoring

An important part of the monitoring process is the attention paid by individual departments and functions of the business to budgets. A budget is a financial plan divided into periods of time (often monthly or four weekly). The budget figures are set for these time periods for a year at a time. As times passes, the actual figures are inserted on a budget report (see fig 1.6 below) and any variances are picked up.

sales budget report (extract)

	period 1			period 2		
	budget £	actual £	variance £	budget £	actual £	variance £
product A	1000	1000	nil	1000	1200	+ 200
product B	1500	1550	+ 50	1500	1500	nil
product C	2500	2200	- 300	2500	2000	- 500
etc . . .						

Fig 1.6 Monitoring of a sales budget

The sales budget report on the previous page is an extract only: it shows two periods and figures for three products. A full-sized budget report is likely to show thirteen four-weekly periods and many more products. The budget has columns for:

- budgeted figures – these will be filled in at the beginning of the year
- actual figures – these will be filled in during the year
- variances – ie the budgeted figures *less* the actual figures

The monitoring process looks at the variances. A *small* variance may not be significant and should be noted by the departmental manager for action (if any) to be taken. A *large* variance may be very significant and should be reported to higher management for a decision to be made. For example:

- a sales figure which is well above target shows that a product is successful – production and advertising should be stepped up so that more can be sold
- a sales figure which is well below target reveals a problem which should be investigated: - is the price too high? - is there a design fault?

Budget monitoring is discussed at greater length in Chapter 6.

chapter summary

■ The business planning and monitoring process is a continuous cycle which involves four stages:
- setting business objectives
- gathering information to assess the situation of the business
- making operational plans and budgets
- monitoring the success of the plans and budgets

■ Business objectives are statements which give the business and its employees a sense of direction and motivation from within. Together they contribute to the long-term strategic *Corporate Plan*, and are often summarised in a short public statement known as the *mission statement*.

■ Business objectives cover areas such as
- profitability
- market share
- product range
- environmental policy
- Human Resources policy

■ Businesses need to collect information in order to be able to formulate plans. This information can be internal or external, or relate to past, present or future.

■ A budget, which forms part of the operational plan, is a plan, usually expressed in financial terms, to enable an objective or a target to be met.

■ The monitoring of operational plans and budgets enables a business to adapt to change and to set new targets.

STUDENT ACTIVITIES

1.1 Consider the ways in which the following businesses operate:
- a car manufacturer
- a food supermarket company
- a hospital
- a fashion clothes manufacturer

and then –

(a)   formulate a mission statement for each of the businesses

(b)   draw up a list of objectives for each business *in order of priority of objective* – remember to give a time limit to the objectives

(c)   point out any conflicts which you see arising out of these objectives

1.2 A large national leisure company is thinking of setting up a ten pin bowling centre in your nearest large town. Write down the types of information that the business will need to gather in order to make a decision. Categorise the information under the following headings:

(a)   external information – past, present and future

(b)   internal information – past, present and future

When you have drawn up your lists, you should, if possible, obtain some of the *external* information which applies to your area, and state how it might affect the decision.

1.3 A friend of yours is confused about business planning. He says that a Corporate Plan, a Business Plan and an operational plan are all one and the same thing. How would you reply? Give detailed reasons for the differences between these three types of plan.

1.4 Someone you know has set up as a sole trader sports shop in the town. He knows a lot about sports equipment, but has less experience of running a business. He is anxious to know how he is getting on, and how well his sales are going. What practical measures could you advise him to take to enable him to monitor his success, and how could these help him in the future?

2 Financial management

introduction

The last chapter looked at the business planning and monitoring process. We saw how a typical business operates by setting objectives, taking stock of its position, and planning ahead. This chapter looks in detail at a how a business is structured so that these decisions can be made. We will concentrate on the 'financial' aspects of management of a business, and will examine:

* *the organisational structure – essentially 'who' makes 'what' decisions*
* *typical job descriptions*
* *committees*
* *relationships between different parts of the business organisation*

organisational structures

types of organisational structure

There are two basic types of organisational structure (illustrated in fig. 2.1 on the opposite page):

the flat structure
The name of the structure is taken from its shape: it is essentially *flat*. The person at the top is in charge of all functions of the business: his or her *span of control* is very wide. You will doubtless be able to apply this type of structure to the sole trader business. The owner will be responsible for business planning, monitoring and budgeting – a fairly demanding role!

the hierarchical structure
A larger business such as a public limited company will have a *hierarchical* structure. A hierarchy is an organisation controlled by levels of authority each with its own responsibilities and functions. The remainder of this chapter will be devoted to describing how the financial planning and monitoring process is carried out in an organisation of this size. Study the business shown in fig. 2.1 before reading on.

a flat structure – showing the functions of the business controlled by a sole trader

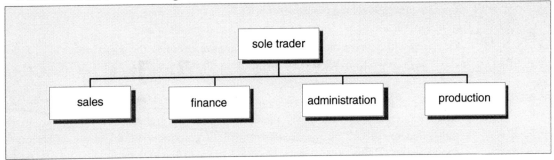

a hierarchical structure – showing the functions of a limited company business and the levels of control

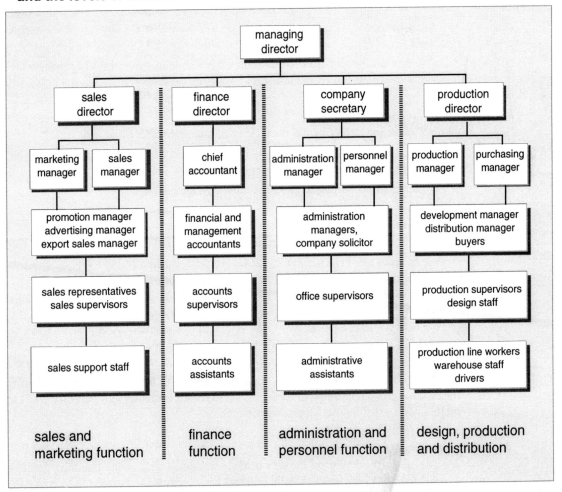

Fig. 2.1 Types of organisational structure

levels of authority

The hierarchical structure illustrated on the previous page is that of a typical public limited company which manufactures a product. It must be stressed that the structure of all organisations will vary to some degree, dependent on

- *size* – the larger the organisation, the more complex the structure
- *nature of the business* – a business providing a service, for example will not have a production department

Whatever the structure looks like, there will be a number of definable levels of authority which have a specific role in the planning and monitoring process. These levels are illustrated in fig. 2.2 on the next page which reproduces the hierarchical structure shown in fig. 2.1, but which omits the details of the different departments and functions. Again we use the example of a public limited company:

board of directors

The board of directors, headed by the managing director, runs the company on behalf of the shareholders. Its role is:

- to set business objectives – the long-term strategic plan (the 'Corporate Plan')
- to appoint the right management team to ensure that the objectives are carried out
- to monitor the situation on a regular basis – normally by means of management reports (produced by departments within the business)

senior management

The directors and departmental managers are together responsible for:

- operational planning – compiling one-year plans which ensure that the business objectives are met in the long-term
- overseeing departmental and functional budgets

middle management

The middle managers are the departmental managers and their assistants. Their role is to:

- ensure the smooth implementation of the operational (one year) plans
- set the departmental budgets – normally for a year at a time – and then monitor them – usually every four weeks, ensuring that targets are met

supervisory management

The role of supervisors and senior clerical staff is to ensure that the operations of the business run smoothly on a day-to-day basis. They will be concerned with ensuring that the business' laid down procedures are followed correctly and that efficiency is maintained so that budget targets can be met.

operational staff

A business must not neglect the role of the operational staff in the planning process. They should be consulted and their suggestions welcomed in helping to improve the efficiency of the business and the quality of the products of the business, a practice used to great effect by the Japanese.

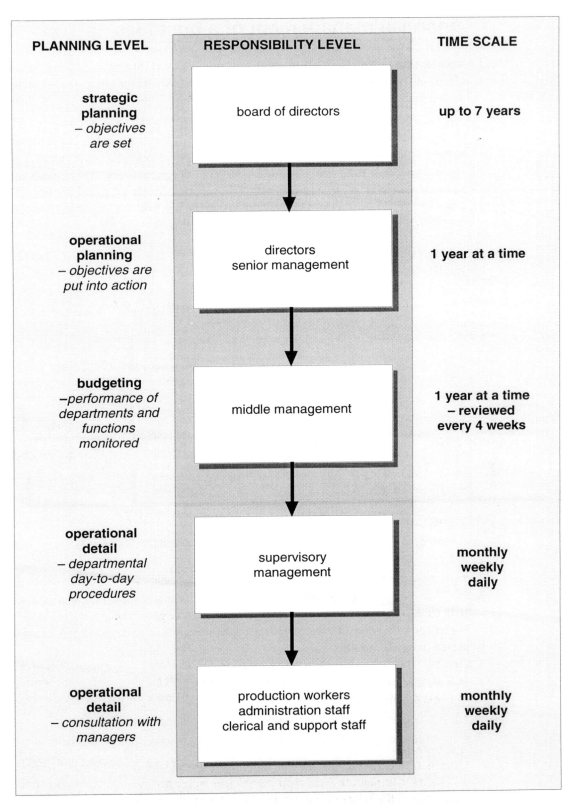

PLANNING LEVEL	RESPONSIBILITY LEVEL	TIME SCALE
strategic planning *– objectives are set*	board of directors	**up to 7 years**
operational planning *– objectives are put into action*	directors senior management	**1 year at a time**
budgeting *–performance of departments and functions monitored*	middle management	**1 year at a time – reviewed every 4 weeks**
operational detail *– departmental day-to-day procedures*	supervisory management	**monthly weekly daily**
operational detail *– consultation with managers*	production workers administration staff clerical and support staff	**monthly weekly daily**

Fig. 2.2 Levels of responsibility in a hierarchical structure

financial management of a business

Now that you have seen the organisational structure as a whole, you will be able to appreciate how the finance function of a business 'fits in' with the other areas of sales, administration and production.

The finance function of the limited company (originally illustrated in fig. 2.1) is shown in its full expanded form in fig. 2.3 below.

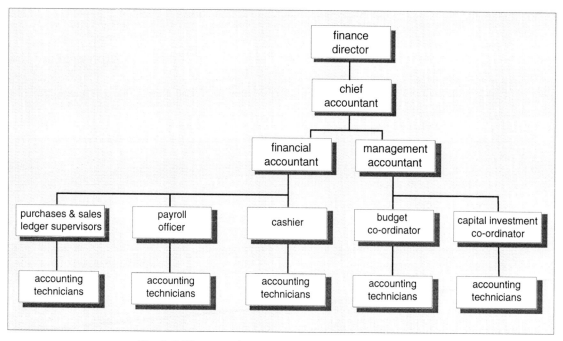

Fig 2.3 Finance department of a limited company

job descriptions

We will now describe the jobs carried out by the various finance department personnel shown in fig. 2.3 above.

finance director

The role of a finance director is

- to help in the formulation of the long-term planning of the business
- to ensure that best use is made of the financial resources of the business
- to monitor the financial performance of the business, eg is it meeting profitability targets?
- to be responsible for the accounting systems and annual statutory accounts of the business

chief accountant

The chief accountant's responsibilities are:

- the overall management of the finance department
- ensuring that financial reports (annual statutory accounts and budget reports) are produced accurately and on time
- recruitment and training of financial staff
- assisting the finance director in long-term planning of the business

The finance department is then divided into two sections headed by the *financial accountant* and the *management accountant*. We will deal with each of these in turn.

financial accountant

The financial accountant's responsibilities are:

- the drawing up of the *financial accounts* accurately and on time – these accounts are the profit statement, the balance sheet and the cashflow statement (please note *not* the cash budget/cash flow forecast – this is drawn up by the management accountant – see below)
- ensuring that the financial accounts comply with all the regulations set down by law, the tax authorities and accountancy bodies
- formulating financial policy, eg when to write off bad debts, how much depreciation to charge on fixed assets such as vehicles and machinery
- supervising staff in the section

purchases ledger supervisor

Purchases ledger (sometimes called 'bought ledger') is the section of the business which deals with recording and paying for goods and services which have been bought from suppliers by the business. The purchases ledger supervisor:

- monitors the accounts of suppliers in the purchases ledger (the *creditors'* accounts)
- ensures that payments are made on time (but not before time!) to creditors

sales ledger supervisor

Sales ledger is the section of the business which deals with recording the accounts of customers to whom goods or services have been supplied (the *debtors'* accounts). The main task is to make sure that customers pay up on time. The supervisor will:

- monitor the accounts of customers (debtors) in the sales ledger
- chase up bad payers
- write off bad debts (ie debtors who are not likely ever to pay)

payroll officer

The payroll officer is in charge of paying the employees of the business. He or she will deal with pay records, tax forms, pension payments, and setting up the payment of wages and salaries.

cashier

The cashier will deal with the keeping of cash within the business, the banking and issue of cheques and the monitoring of the bank account.

management accountant

The management accountant and the staff he or she controls, deals with both

- *cost accounting* – calculating how much it costs to make a product or provide a service, and also
- *management accounting* – the planning and monitoring process of preparing budgets and assessing capital investment projects

The responsibilities of the management accountant are:

- calculating costs for products and services
- preparing budgets, liaising with the finance director, chief accountant, the financial accountant and departmental managers
- monitoring expenditure against the various budgets and reporting major variances (eg sales revenue 20% down on target, wages costs 10% more than budget)
- investigating the cause of major variances and advising departmental heads on corrective action
- assessing capital investment projects – eg should the business buy new computers?

budget co-ordinator

The budget co-ordinator acts as a go-between for all concerned in the budgeting process. He or she liaises, advises, co-ordinates and communicates between the senior management and the departmental heads. See page 30 for a fuller explanation.

Note: this role is often taken by the management accountant or a member of his team.

capital investment co-ordinator

The capital investment co-ordinator acts in a similar way to the budget co-ordinator except that the task undertaken is the forward planning of capital (long-term/permanent) investment, eg a new warehouse, a production line, a fleet of cars.

Note: this role is often taken by the management accountant or a member of his team.

accounting technicians

The accounting technicians (or accounting 'assistants') carry out under supervision the day-to-day work of the finance department, eg the recording of financial transactions.

responsibilities within the organisation

relationships within the organisational structure

The organisational structures illustrated so far in this chapter show that authority and control are exercised from above, and pass down through the levels of the hierarchy. This is known as a *line relationship*.

line relationships

In any organisation a clear line of authority and responsibility can be traced from the top to the bottom of the hierarchy:

- policy and instructions pass downwards
- responsibility for actions, errors and complaints passes upwards
- responsibility for decisions can be delegated downwards

The financial and management accountants, for example are directly responsible to the finance director and chief accountant for the implementation of financial policy. They may be called to report to the board of directors on specific issues.

Although the line relationship is the most obvious relationship, there are also other relationships not shown on the charts. These include *advisory* (or 'staff') relationships and *function* relationships (see fig. 2.4)

advisory relationships

An advisory (or 'staff') relationship exists when, say, a manager is given advice by someone else, possibly a staff member working in another department who does not have a line relationship with that manager. The manager accepts responsibility for all decisions taken as a result of that advice; the adviser is free of responsibility. For example, the sales manager (sales & marketing department) may call upon the sales ledger supervisor (finance department) to provide a list of bad payers, so that the sales representatives are warned about selling to people who have not paid for goods previously ordered.

function relationships

A function relationship is established when a person is appointed as a specialist to carry out a specific function within an organisation, and takes responsibility for that function. A specialist will be responsible to the senior management (eg directors) and will relieve a line manager of that responsibility. For example if the finance department is being re-organised, a systems analyst and a computer consultant may be brought in to advise the choice and implementation of computer systems. The financial and management accountants will liaise with them, but will not ultimately be responsible for the decisions made.

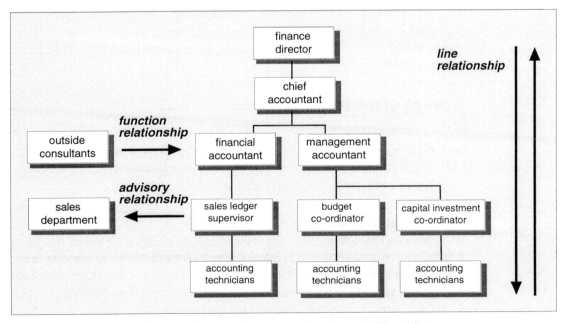

Fig 2.4 Line, advisory and function relationships

committees

the function of committees

A committee is a group of people brought together for a specific purpose. A committee may be:

- an *ad hoc* committee, ie a temporary 'one-off' committee for a specific occasion, event or purpose – for example a business investigating a new project, or your student group planning a foreign trip
- a formal committee, ie a permanent group established as part of the way an organisation functions and communicates – for example, a budget committee, a school or college staff/student committee

A committee often (but not always) brings together people who do not normally work together, for example employees from different departments, employees from different levels of management.

It has often been said by critics of committees that a camel is a horse designed by a committee! Committees certainly have their advantages and disadvantages:

advantages of committees

- expertise brought together within an organisation
- communication between different departments and levels of management
- shared responsibility for decisions

disadvantages of committees

- committees can be great time wasters
- committees can get too large and unmanageable

A properly constituted committee should have a chairman, a secretary, clear terms of reference, and minutes circulated in advance. Its decisions should be unambiguous and acted upon.

types of committee

There are a number of different committees which deal with financial decisions:

- the board of directors is itself a governing committee
- cost reduction committees – involving different departments
- budget committees – explained in detail below

the budget committee

We have seen when explaining the role of the management accountant that the budgeting process involves many different people and areas of responsibility within the business: directors, senior managers and departmental heads. The work of the budget committee is facilitated by the budget co-ordinator, often the management accountant.

Study fig. 2.5 on the next page and read the text that follows.

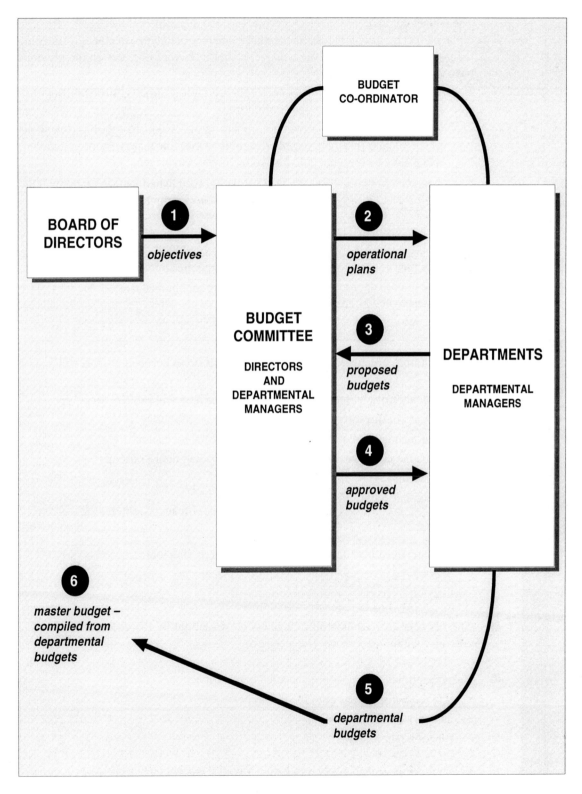

Fig. 2.5 Workings of the budget committee

The budget committee is made up of directors and departmental managers. The role of the budget co-ordinator – often the management accountant – is pivotal in keeping the process together and 'on the rails'. The stages shown in fig. 2.5 on the previous page are as follows:

1. The objectives of the business (eg products, markets, profitability) are communicated to the budget committee.

2. The budget committee draws up 12 month operational plans – the basic elements of the budgets (normally supplied in draft form by the management accountant) and passes them to the individual departmental managers.

3. The departmental managers, in consultation with their supervisors, convert the draft plans into proposed budgets and submit them to the budget committee. They are then scrutinised by the committee and checked to see if they will 'work' together. They may be passed back to the departments for amendment and redrafting before final approval by the committee.

4. The final versions of the departmental budgets are approved and put into action.

5. The finance department then compiles the master budget from all the subsidiary departmental budgets (see Chapter 5).

chapter summary

- Organisational structures may be flat, or – as with larger businesses – hierarchical.

- Levels of authority within a limited company business will probably include:
  - the board of directors
  - senior management – directors and departmental managers
  - middle management – departmental managers and their assistants
  - supervisors
  - operational staff

- Planning responsibilities are as follows:
  - strategic planning (up to 7 years) – the board of directors
  - operational planning (1 year) – senior management
  - budgeting (1 year) – middle management

- The financial management of a business is carried out by the different levels of authority within the Finance Department.

- Responsibilities within the organisation can involve:
  - line relationships
  - advisory relationships
  - function relationships

- Committees are a means of co-ordinating financial management across the structure of a business – the budget committee, for example.

STUDENT ACTIVITIES

2.1 Draw up structure charts for the following types of business:

(a) sole trader

(b) partnership

(c) limited company

Where possible, base your evidence on real businesses in your area. Your tutor should be able to arrange introductions to local Chambers of Commerce and TECs.

If you live in an area where this is not possible, base your findings on readings of texts in Resource Centres – the topic of business structure forms part of your 'Business Systems' studies.

2.2 At what level of authority within a limited company business would you expect to deal with the decisions and actions listed below? Choose from:

- board level
- senior management
- middle management
- supervisory level
- operational staff

(a) planning to raise more money by a new issue of shares

(b) sending out a standard reminder letter to a customer who has not paid an invoice

(c) drawing up the financial element of an operational plan

(d) setting a departmental budget

(e) printing out the monthly customer statements

2.3 A friend of yours is interested in going into financial management. Advise him or her by

(a) drawing up a job description of
 – an accounting technician
 – a finance director

(b) researching the qualifications that will be needed in both these roles, and where they can be obtained

Suggested sources of evidence include businesses in your area, local careers libraries, Jobcentres and the professional Accountancy bodies.

2.4 State whether the following activities involve a *line*, *advisory* or *function* relationship:

(a) the financial director calls on the purchasing manager to ask about the cost of raw materials

(b) the management accountant has a meeting with the budget co-ordinator

(c) an accounting technician suggests to his supervisor a better way of monitoring the cost of stationery used by the business

(d) the board of directors employs a systems analyst to look at the running of the Finance Department

(e) the financial accountant discusses with the sales manager how they can interchange information held on the firms's computer about customers' buying habits

2.5 State:

(a) how committees can help and hinder the efficient running of a business – use any committee of which you have experience to illustrate your points

(b) how a budget co-ordinator in a limited company business bridges the gaps between the different levels of authority and enables the budget committee to function effectively

Financial management in local organisations

for BTEC Element 11.1
*Explain the need for financial information as part of business
planning and monitoring activity*

INTRODUCTION

This Evidence Collection Exercise requires you to investigate two local organisations, and to write a report which compares:

- the way the organisations use financial information in the planning process
- the objectives of the organisations
- the structure of the organisations
- the way in which financial management operates in the organisations

TASKS

You are to choose two local organisations for investigation. It is recommended that the two chosen types are very different in what they do and how they are structured. For example you might choose two from:

- a public limited company in your area – this could either be a company based in your area, or a branch, shop or office of a business which operates on a national basis
- a local partnership – either a business which manufactures a product, or a business which provides a service (eg a firm of accountants)
- a local school, sixth form college or college of further education

You are to compile a formal written report which should cover the following areas:

1. **information needed by the organisation**

   Identify and give examples (where possible) of the types of information which each organisation will need in the planning process.

   For example:

   - who are the customers?
   - what competition exists?
   - how successful is the organisation in comparison with the competition?
   - what physical resources – eg premises, equipment – are needed?
   - how is the workforce made up and where does it come from?
   - what political and economic factors could affect the organisation?

   Show how this information helps in the business planning process.

2. **statement of objectives**

   Investigate and compare where possible the mission statement and corporate objectives (or equivalent) of each organisation.

   If there is no published mission statement or set of objectives for either organisation, *draft your own* and try to obtain some feedback from the organisation(s) about what you have written.

3. **structure of financial management**

   (a) Draw up a structure plan for each organisation, paying particular attention where possible to the financial management of the organisation.

   (b) Compare the two structure plans. What conclusions about the financial management of the organisation can you draw from your comparison? What examples of line, function and advisory relationships can you find?

NOTE
It would be useful for this and the other Evidence Collection Exercises if the school or college could make contact with a number of local business organisations in order to obtain information, arrange visits and talks, and generally foster links with business. In this way the objectives of the GNVQ Award will be fully realised.

Section

2

budgeting

3 Setting the budgets

introduction

This chapter examines the way a business sets up its budgeting system. We will:

- *define a budget*
- *explain the purpose of budgeting*
- *examine the different types of budget*

We will then set out in a Case Study how a manufacturing business sets the following budgets:

- *sales budget – what can the business sell in the next 12 months?*
- *production budget – how can the business make all the items it plans to sell?*
- *staffing budget – what is the cost of the staff needed by the business?*

The cash budget, which forecasts the flows of money in and out of the bank account, will be explained in Chapter 4, and the master budget – a summary of all the budgets to provide projected financial statements, ie a profit statement and a balance sheet, will be examined in Chapter 5.

budgets explained

a definition

It is useful at this point to remind ourselves of what a budget is:

A budget is a means of planning and control used by the management of a business to achieve stated objectives

A budget is commonly set in financial terms, eg a sales revenue budget, but it can also be expressed in terms of units, eg items produced, workers employed, items sold.

Budgets can be *income* budgets for money received by the business (eg a sales budget) or *expenditure* budgets for money spent (eg a staffing budget).

timescale

Most budgets are prepared for the forthcoming financial year, and are usually broken down into shorter time periods, commonly four-weekly. This enables control to be exercised over the budget: as time passes, so the business' actual results can be monitored against the budget, and discrepancies between the two can be investigated.

benefits of budgets

Budgets provide benefits both for the business, and also for its managers:

assisting decision making

Budgets help the management of businesses to see the outcome of different courses of action and to make decisions accordingly.

motivating staff

Budgets motivate staff by setting targets which have to be met. This can, of course, only take place if the targets are realistic!

measuring performance

Budgets enable businesses to see how successful they are in meeting targets, eg sales, production, staff costs.

types of budget

Budgets are subdivided into two main types: the *function* budget and the *departmental* budget.

function budget

The function budget is a plan for a specific *function* within a business, eg:

- sales budget – which covers sales income to be received by the business
- production budget – which covers the number of items produced and their cost
- staffing budget – which plans the wages and salaries cost of the entire workforce

departmental budget

The costs of running a business set out in the function budgets are also included by its operating departments in *departmental budgets*, eg sales department budget administration department budget. The object here is to make each department run efficiently: its managers – known as the *budget holders* – will be set specific targets for spending and productivity in terms of staffing and spending, for example. Responsibility for less important areas of spending will fall on the supervisors. The end result should be that the staff are motivated to achieve the targets that are set.

Both function and departmental budgets are described as *subsidiary* budgets, ie they are subsidiary to the master budget, and are combined to produce the figures for the master budget (see fig. 3.1 on page 39).

the master budget

The end result of the budgeting process is the production of a *master budget* which takes the form of forecast operating statements – an estimated profit statement and balance sheet at the end of the budget period. The master budget is the 'master plan' which shows how all the subsidiary budgets 'work together'. The subsidiary budgets include:

- departmental budgets and function budgets
- a cash budget – which will show money paid in and out of the bank account
- a capital budget – which will plan for large items of expenditure

Look now at fig. 3.1 on the next page, which shows how all the budgets are related to each other.

In this chapter we will explain by means of a Case Study the sales, production and staffing budgets. The cash budget and master budget are discussed more fully in Chapters 4 and 5.

limiting factors

A limiting factor is some aspect of the business which prevents further expansion.

All budgets are affected by *limiting factors;* these factors include:

- the quantity of a product which can be sold – this principle applies whether the 'product' is a manufactured item or a service
- the availability of raw materials
- the availability of skilled labour
- factory or office space
- finance

It is essential to identify the limiting factor(s). For most businesses the limiting factor will be *sales*. The starting point for the budgeting process is therefore normally the *sales budget.* Consequently the order in which the budgets will be drafted is often:

- *sales budget –* what can the business sell in the next 12 months?
- *production budget –* how can the business make all the items which it plans to sell?
- *staffing, purchases and overheads budgets –* what resources in terms of labour and raw materials will the business need to produce the items? – what other expenses will be incurred?
- *departmental budgets –* what resources will be needed by individual departments?
- *capital budget –* what fixed assets (eg machinery, vehicles) need to be purchased over the next 12 months?
- *cash budget –* what money will be flowing in and out of the bank account? – will an overdraft be needed?
- *master budget –* a summary of all the budgets to provide projected financial statements, ie a profit statement and balance sheet

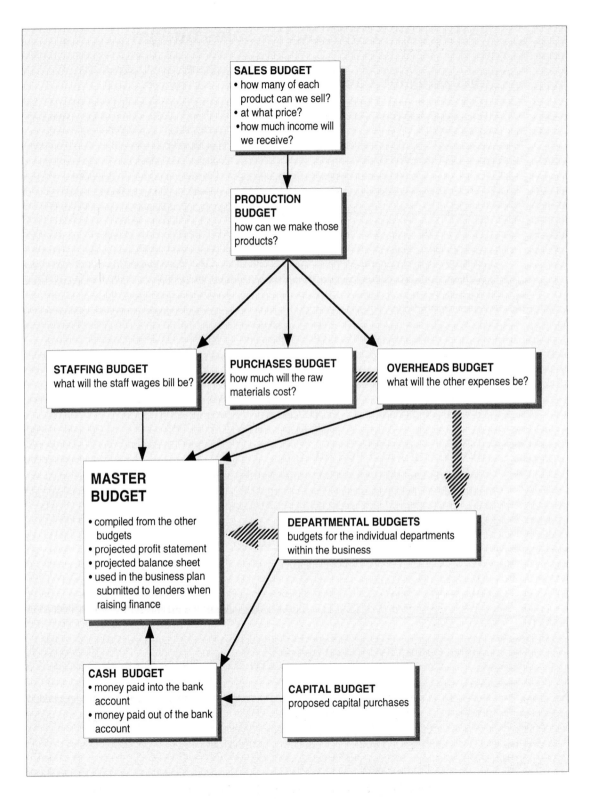

Fig. 3.1 The budgeting process

structure of a budget – sales budget

gathering information

The sales budget is the starting point for any type of business. It is an annual plan which will project the sales of:

- products made by a *manufacturing* business, eg cars, CDs, tubes of toothpaste, breakfast cereals

- services provided by a *service* business – eg holidays, educational courses, train journeys, insurance policies, haircuts

The *accuracy* of the sales budget is critical for the success of the business. If a business overestimates sales it will be left with – using the examples given above – surplus cars, empty trains, or idle hairdressers. If it underestimates sales it could have to turn customers away. Both ways it could lose money. Of course budgeting is not a precise science and a business would be unlikely to achieve 100% accuracy. It is essential however that as much *accurate information* as possible is gathered. This can include:

- details of past sales performance – available within the business

- present sales figures – up-to-date figures from sales representatives

- what the competition is doing – estimates of market share

- assessment of whether the market is expanding or declining

- forecasts made – by sales representatives and by market researchers

- trading conditions – the UK and world economic climate

analysing the sales budget

A sales budget will start off by projecting the number of units to be sold over a year and then applying a selling price to produce an estimate of the income figure in money terms. There is no laid-down format for a sales budget: it can project sales in a number of different ways:

- by product

- by customer (or type of customer)

- by geographical area

Study the following examples which illustrate each of the three formats:

sales budget by product (extract)							
	January	February	March	April	May	June	Total
	£	£	£	£	£	£	£
product A	1,000	1,000	1,000	1,000	1,000	1,000	6,000
product B	1,500	1,500	1,500	1,500	1,500	1,500	9,000
product C	2,500	2,500	2,500	2,500	2,500	2,500	15,000
etc ...							

sales budget by customer (extract)

	January £	February £	March £	April £	May £	June £	Total £
Direct sales	10,000	10,000	10,000	12,000	12,000	12,000	66,000
Agency sales	5,000	5,000	5,000	5,000	5,000	5,000	30,000
Mail order	5,000	5,000	6,000	5,000	6,000	6,000	33,000
etc . . .							

sales budget by geographical area (extract)

	January £M	February £M	March £M	April £M	May £M	June £M	Total £M
UK sales	40	40	50	40	40	50	260
EU sales	50	50	50	50	50	50	300
USA sales	10	10	15	10	10	15	70
etc . . .							

structure of a budget

Certain aspects of the structure of the sales budget (and any budget) will stay constant, whether they are income budgets or expenditure budgets:

budget periods

The budget is subdivided into 'budget periods': either months or four-weekly periods (the 52 week year is conveniently divided into 13 four-weekly periods). The extracts above show six of the usual twelve monthly periods.

budget heads

The subdivision of the budget by product (or any other category of income or expense) is known as a 'budget head'. If the budget is an expenses budget, this head will be known as an 'expense head', eg telephone costs, insurance, wages.

setting the production budget

When a business has established its sales budget ('How many of each product can we sell?') it is then in a position to work out its production budget ('How can we make those products on time?'). It must be stressed that a *production* budget applies to a *manufacturing* business; a business providing a *service* will carry out a similar process using an *operating* budget.

gathering information

When setting a production budget, the management of a business must gather together information about its resources and consider a range of external factors in order to assess what it can and cannot achieve. Factors include:

timing	When during the year are the products required? Are there any seasonal fluctuations which will produce uneven demands on production facilities? Will the business therefore need to hold any stock of products in advance?
capacity	Can the existing production facilities cope with the expected demand? Will new machines be necessary? Should the business subcontract work to other manufacturers?
labour cost	Does the business have the right number of production staff? Will it need more staff? Should it introduce an additional shift? Would it be better to pay existing staff overtime?
materials	Can the business obtain the right quality of materials at the right price?

When all this information has been gathered and analysed, the business should then be in a position to set an annual production budget, taking into account:

* the projected monthly sales figures
* the finished products in stock at the beginning and end of each month

production budget for 199-

UNITS	Jan	Feb	Mar	Apr	May	Jun	Jul	Aug	Sep	Oct	Nov	Dec
Opening stock	100	275	450	600	550	500	450	300	175	325	475	125
add Units produced	325	325	350	350	350	350	350	175	350	350	350	400
less Units sold	150	150	200	400	400	400	500	300	200	200	700	425
Closing stock	275	450	600	550	500	450	300	175	325	475	125	100

units and cost

You will see from the production budget set out above that it is expressed in terms of *units of production*. When the monthly production of units has been calculated, the budget can then be expressed in money terms – it will become a *production cost budget* This will be made possible by applying a *standard cost* worked out by the business from the raw materials cost, the labour cost and the overheads (other expenses) which were needed to manufacture a single unit of production. Note that overheads can be:

fixed – ie they will not vary with the level of production, eg business rates

variable – ie they will vary with the level of production, eg selling expenses

setting the staffing budget

The staffing budget of a business is a *function* budget: it calculates the staffing needs and costs of *all* departments within the business and is compiled in consultation with departmental managers. A staffing budget is more difficult to 'get right' than some other budgets. Employees tend to be permanent and require a relatively fixed rate of pay. If business is quiet at a particular time of the year, and the staffing needs are reduced, the management cannot easily say 'we will reduce the number of employees this month' or 'we will pay them less this month.' One solution is to employ temporary or part-time staff. The staffing budget therefore needs careful planning.

staffing expense heads

The categories of staffing expense are as follows:

gross pay	The amount of money paid to each employee – normally based on an annual amount, for example a director earning £30,000 a year. This the amount which the business will have to pay, although of course the employee will receive a *net* amount after deductions of tax and National Insurance.
National Insurance	The employer has to pay National Insurance Contributions *in addition to* the employee's contribution. This is calculated as a percentage (commonly 10.2%) of gross pay.
pension payments	Many employers contribute to the pension schemes of the employees, paying, for example 5% of gross pay.
benefits in kind	Employers sometime reward more senior employees with *benefits in kind* (perks) such as company cars, health insurance.

As staffing expenses are reasonably steady over the course of the year, the procedure is often for the *annual* figures for each expense head to be divided by twelve to produce the monthly figure. A typical staffing budget would appear as follows (extract for six months shown):

staffing budget (extract)						
	January	February	March	April	May	June
	£	£	£	£	£	£
Gross pay	40,000	40,000	40,000	40,000	40,000	40,000
National Insurance	4,080	4,080	4,080	4,080	4,080	4,080
Pension payments	2,000	2,000	2,000	2,000	2,000	2,000
etc . . .						

There now follows a Case Study which illustrates the budget setting process in a limited company manufacturing business. The setting up of a sales budget is followed by the production budget and the staffing budget.

CASE STUDY
BUDGET SETTING – FITTA HOMEGYM LIMITED

Fitta Homegym Limited has just finished its first year in business. It has a single very successful product – the Fitta 'Homegym', a set of body-building and fitness equipment for use in the home. The selling price of the 'Homegym' is £1,000. Sales for the first year of trading have been excellent, and were helped greatly by an advertising campaign in November, aimed at the Christmas present market. So far the business has not established a formal budgeting system.

setting the sales budget
Wayne Dayley, the Managing Director, is considering with Tom Edwards (Finance Director) and Ben James (Production Director) the projected sales for the coming year. His accountant has advised them to set up a budgeting system, starting with a sales budget. He is therefore looking closely at the resources of the business and other data relating to sales. The information he has available is as follows:

- *first year's sales (by month)*

January	100 units
February	100 units
March	150 units
April	350 units
May	350 units
June	350 units
July	450 units
August	250 units
September	150 units
October	150 units
November	500 units
December	375 units

- *current sales trends*
The two sales representatives report a healthy level of sales for the time of year.

- *competitor activity*
Other businesses are active in the gym equipment area. Wayne notes that his main competitor has recently reduced the price of their 'home gym' to £1,100.

- *consumer buying habits*
The trend for healthy living continues, and economic indicators show that consumers have money to spend on leisure activities. Statistics also show that they also have more leisure time, and forecasts suggest that this trend will continue.

The questions facing Wayne and his directors are therefore:
* how many Homegyms can we sell this year?
* what is the seasonal pattern of sales?
* what price should we charge?

• sales volume

The sales representatives report that they can sell an extra 50 units a month on current demand – the factory has actually been out of stock at times during the year. The sales manager adds that sales are seasonal: with more advertising in the autumn they could sell an additional 200 units in November (this includes the extra 50 already mentioned). The projected sales (by unit) are therefore:

January	100	+ 50	= 150 units
February	100	+ 50	= 150 units
March	150	+ 50	= 200 units
April	350	+ 50	= 400 units
May	350	+ 50	= 400 units
June	350	+ 50	= 400 units
July	450	+ 50	= 500 units
August	250	+ 50	= 300 units
September	150	+ 50	= 200 units
October	150	+ 50	= 200 units
November	500	+ 200	= 700 units
December	375	+ 50	= 425 units

• setting a price

The directors decide to keep the selling price at its current level of £1,000, despite a 5% increase in raw materials cost. The reasons for this are that:

- this will still undercut the nearest competitor's price of £1,100
- Tom, the finance director, calculates there is sufficient profit margin
- a low price should stimulate sales

Sales income is therefore budgeted at:

January	150 units x £1,000	=	£150,000
February	150 units x £1,000	=	£150,000
March	200 units x £1,000	=	£200,000
April	400 units x £1,000	=	£400,000
May	400 units x £1,000	=	£400,000
June	400 units x £1,000	=	£400,000
July	500 units x £1,000	=	£500,000
August	300 units x £1,000	=	£300,000
September	200 units x £1,000	=	£200,000
October	200 units x £1,000	=	£200,000
November	700 units x £1,000	=	£700,000
December	425 units x £1,000	=	£425,000
TOTAL SALES	4,025 units x £1,000	=	£4,025,000

This level of budgeted sales is considered to be realistic, and the final sales budget is completed and the monthly budget columns filled in (note the breakdown between retail sales to shops and direct mail order). The full 12 month budget will be a large sheet or computer printout showing columns for 12 months: here we illustrate the first six months only.

FITTA HOMEGYM LTD – SALES BUDGET (extract)

	January	February	March	April	May	June	Total
	£	£	£	£	£	£	£
Retail sales	100,000	100,000	150,000	300,000	300,000	300,000	1,250,000
Mail order	50,000	50,000	50,000	100,000	100,000	100,000	450,000
TOTAL SALES	150,000	150,000	200,000	400,000	400,000	400,000	1,700,000

setting the production budget

Now that the sales budget is set, Ben, the production director, can calculate how he is going to produce the appropriate number of units each month. He has the following limiting factors to bear in mind:

- Stock in the warehouse on 1 January is 100 units.
- Ben's problem is that the factory, working at normal capacity, can produce 350 units each month. More units can be made if overtime is paid, but the directors are not keen to see this happen, just as they do not like to see too much under-utilisation of the factory. Ben has to work out an even production budget which will keep the factory working at near or full capacity, but without incurring too much overtime.
- Month-end stock must never fall below 100 units (to avoid the shortages experienced last year)
- The warehouse is fairly small and cannot hold more than 600 units.
- The factory is closed for half of August for the annual holidays.

Ben calculates the following production schedule for the year:

FITTA HOMEGYM LTD – PRODUCTION BUDGET

UNITS	Jan	Feb	Mar	Apr	May	Jun	Jul	Aug	Sep	Oct	Nov	Dec
Opening stock	100	275	450	600	550	500	450	300	175	325	475	125
add Units produced	325	325	350	350	350	350	350	175	350	350	350	400
less Units sold	150	150	200	400	400	400	500	300	200	200	700	425
Closing stock	275	450	600	550	500	450	300	175	325	475	125	100

Note that Ben has been successful in meeting all the limiting factors, except that:

- the factory will under-produce by 25 units in both January and February
- overtime will have to be paid for the production of 50 units in December

setting the staffing budget

Fitta Homegym Limited is a relatively small company. The employees and their expenses are as follows:

directors
There are three directors, each earning £25,000 a year. The company contributes to a pension scheme for each of them (5% of gross pay).

managers
There are ten managers, each earning on average £15,000 a year. The same pension arrangements apply (5% of gross pay paid by the company).

other staff
There are 50 other employees, each earning on average £8,000 a year. The company makes no contribution to their pension scheme.

The staffing expenses are therefore:

directors (3)	gross pay	£75,000
	National Insurance	£7,650
	pensions	£3,750

managers (10)	gross pay	£150,000
	National Insurance	£15,300
	pensions	£7,500

other staff (50)	gross pay	£400,000
	National Insurance	£40,800

From these annual figures the staffing budget is then drawn up by dividing each expense head annual figure by twelve, ie:

- all items for gross pay (£625,000 per year, £52,083 per month)
- all items for National Insurance (£63,750 per year, £5,313 per month)
- all items for pensions (£11,250 per year, £938 per month)

FITTA HOMEGYM LTD – STAFFING BUDGET (extract)

	January	February	March	April	May	June
	£	£	£	£	£	£
Gross pay	52,083	52,083	52,083	52,083	52,083	52,083
National Insurance	5,313	5,313	5,313	5,313	5,313	5,313
Pension contributions	938	938	938	938	938	938
TOTAL	58,334	58,334	58,334	58,334	58,334	58,334

setting the other budgets

In this Case Study we have looked at the sales, production and staffing budgets of Fitta Homegym Limited. All three will contribute to the master budget and the cash budget – which we will explain in the next two chapters.

It should be noted that other budgets will also be drawn up (which fall outside the scope of this chapter). These cover areas such as:

- *purchases* – the cost of raw materials and stock which are used in the production process; these appear as 'cost of sales' in the profit statement in the master budget
- *overheads* – other expenses incurred by the business such as rates, insurance, and fuel bills; these appear in the projected profit statement in the master budget

monitoring the budgets

As the year progresses, separate budget reports are prepared monthly. The 'actual' and 'variance'columns are filled in and cumulative figures (ie the year-to-date figures) are calculated and entered in the columns on the right-hand side. A computer spreadsheet will often be used for this task. In the illustration below, the business has reached the end of December with different sales figures from those projected at the beginning of the year. What do you think will be the reaction of the directors?

FITTA HOMEGYM LTD – SALES BUDGET REPORT (extract)

	December			Year-to-date		
	budget	actual	variance	budget	actual	variance
	£	£	£	£	£	£
Retail sales	200,000	250,000	+ 50,000	2,750,000	3,125,000	+ 375,000
Mail order	225,000	200,000	– 25,000	1,275,000	1,350,000	+ 75,000
TOTAL SALES	425,000	450,000	+ 25,000	4,025,000	4,475,000	+ 450,000

• *variances*

The directors will be monitoring the budget during the year and will be watching closely the differences between the budgeted and actual figures – the *variances* shown in the 'variance' column. Note that there are two types of variance:

- a *favourable variance* (results are better than expected) indicated here with a + sign (alternatively the abbreviation 'FAV' could be used)
- an *adverse variance* (results are worse than expected) indicated here with a – sign (alternatively the abbreviation 'ADV' could be used, or the figure placed in brackets)

The directors in this case should be well pleased with the sales results. We will look in more detail at the budget monitoring process in Chapter 6.

■ Budgets help managers to plan and control the operation of the business.

■ Budgets can be:
  • income or expenditure budgets
  • function or departmental budgets

■ Budgets are affected by limiting factors, eg the amount of products that can be sold, factory space, finance.

■ Individual budgets – subsidiary budgets – all contribute to the master budget.

■ Budgets involve planning,(ie target setting), and control,ie the monitoring of how those targets are met.

■ A sales budget projects the number of products that can be sold in a given period and sets a price, so that income can be forecast.

■ A production budget is a plan showing how the production facilities can meet the requirements of the sales targets, ie how the products can be made, and when.

■ A staffing budget sets out the annual cost of employing the staff needed by the business in terms of gross pay, National Insurance, pensions and other benefits.

STUDENT ACTIVITIES

3.1 Explain the differences between

(a) a function budget

(b) a departmental budget

(c) a master budget

3.2 Enigma Books Limited publishes textbooks which it sells to schools and colleges throughout the UK. The company is currently producing budgets for the next year. The sales director is budgeting for sales of 96,000 books:

• the selling price is £10 each

• 75% of annual sales are made in the months of June, July, August and September (spread evenly over all four months)

• the remaining sales are spread evenly over the other eight months

A general election was announced a few days ago, and conversation at today's board meeting of the company's directors went as follows:

"The outcome of the election looks unpredictable."

"If the government is re-elected, they are committed to a 10% cut in education spending."

"On the other hand, if the opposition party win, they have pledged to increase education spending by 25%."

"Until we get further information we had better assume that our sales will be affected by the same percentages."

As an accounts assistant, you are to:

(a)   Prepare a monthly sales budget for the year based on sales of 96,000 books.

(b)   Prepare two further monthly sales budgets based on the percentage changes in educational spending proposed by each of the main political parties.

3.3   Bowdecker Limited is a small business which produces guidebooks for the tourist centres of the Midlands.   At present it publishes four titles, all of which sell at £10 each.

The Cotswolds	(30% of sales)
Worcester and the Malverns	(20% of sales)
Stratford-upon-Avon	(35% of sales)
Living Industrial Heritage	(15% of sales)

The sales outlets are:

Bookshops	75% of sales(£)
Mail order	20% of sales(£)
Library supply firms	5% of sales(£)

Sales for 19-1 were:

January	£10,000	July	£30,000
February	£10,000	August	£35,000
March	£15,000	September	£25,000
April	£20,000	October	£20,000
May	£25,000	November	£10,000
June	£30,000	December	£10,000

The cost of producing the 24,000 books sold in 19-1 were:

Item cost – including materials, labour and variable overheads: £5 per book

Fixed costs (costs that do not vary, regardless of the number of books produced): £48,000

Assuming that Bowdecker Limited continues to produce the four guidebooks, you are to:

(a)   State what factors may affect the level of sales in 19-2.

(b)   Draw up sales budgets for 19-2 showing a breakdown of monthly sales:

   – by product

   – by sales outlet

You estimate that sales will increase by 10% in 19-2.

(c)   Assuming that fixed costs will remain at £48,000 in 19-2 and variable costs at £5 per book, calculate the profit generated by the 10% increase in sales. What is the percentage increase in profit? Why is it not 10%?

3.4   Swing Products makes surfboards. The sales budget for 19-2 is as follows:

January	200 units
February	200 units
March	300 units
April	700 units
May	700 units
June	900 units
July	900 units
August	900 units
September	300 units
October	300 units
November	200 units
December	200 units

- stock in the warehouse at the beginning of January is 200 units

- stock must not fall below 200 units

- maximum production per month is 700 units

- the warehouse cannot hold more than 1500 units

You are to

(a)   Draw up a production budget for 19-2, bearing in mind all the above limiting factors.

(b)   Suggest ways in which the management of Alpha Products could solve the production problem which might occur at the end of the year.

3.5   Swing Products is also planning its staff costs for 19-2. The employees and their pay details are as follows:

employee	number	salary	National Insurance	pension
directors	4	£30,000	10.2% of pay	5% of pay
managers	5	£22,000	10.2% of pay	5% of pay
supervisors	15	£18,000	10.2% of pay	5% of pay
production staff	40	£12,000	10.2% of pay	none
clerical staff	25	£10,000	10.2% of pay	none

You are to draw up a staffing budget for Swing Products for the twelve months of 19-2.

4 The cash budget

introduction

In this chapter we turn to a specific type of budget – the cash budget – which forecasts the flow of money in and out of the bank account of the business. Another name for the cash budget is the 'cash flow forecast.'

We examine, partly by means of a Case Study:
- *the function of the cash budget*
- *the format of the cash budget*
- *the way the cash budget can be set out in a computer spreadsheet program*

function of the cash budget

We have already seen in the last two chapters how the budgeting process involves the drawing up of *subsidiary budgets* (eg sales, production, staffing) leading to the compilation of a *master budget*. The master budget gives the whole picture of how the business should operate over a twelve month period. It projects a *profit statement* by setting budgeted expenses (eg purchases, overheads) against budgeted sales (the sales budget). It also projects a *balance sheet* to show the assets (items owned) and liabilities (amounts owed) at the end of the twelve month period.

Part of the process leading to the master budget is the *cash budget*. This shows projections of money received and money spent over the year passing through the bank account, eg sales income, runnning expenses, payment of tax, purchase of capital items. It is an important budget because:
- it shows when the business may need to borrow from the bank
- it shows the effect on the bank account of the business of a given rise or fall in income or expenses

format of the cash budget

The purpose of a typical cash budget is to set out:

- the expected bank account receipts and payments
- on a month-by-month basis
- for a twelve month period

This is done in order to show the estimated bank balance at the end of each month throughout the period. From the cash budget, the managers of a business can decide what action to take when a surplus of cash is shown to be available or, as is more likely, when a bank overdraft needs to be arranged. A simplified format of a cash budget, with sample figures, is set out below.

Name ....Cash Budget for the .... months ending				
	Jan £000	Feb £000	Mar £000	etc. £000
Receipts				
eg sales receipts	150	150	161	170
other receipts (loans, capital, interest)	70	80	75	80
Total receipts for month (A)	220	230	236	250
Payments				
eg to creditors	160	165	170	170
expenses	50	50	50	60
fixed assets		50		
Total payments for month (B)	210	265	220	230
Net cash flow (Receipts less Payments, ie A-B)	10	(35)	16	20
Add bank balance at beginning of month	10	20	(15)	1
Bank balance (overdraft) at end of month	20	(15)	1	21

As you can see, the cash budget consists of three main sections:

Receipts are analysed for each month to show the amount that is expected to be received from sources such as cash sales, receipts from customers supplied on credit, sale of fixed assets, loans, capital introduced and any interest or other income received.

Payments will show how much is expected to be paid each month for cash purchases, to creditors (suppliers), running expenses, purchases of fixed assets, repayment of capital and loans, interest paid and VAT and other tax paid.

Bank summary at the bottom of the budget shows net cash flow (total receipts less total payments) added to the bank balance at the beginning of the month, resulting in the estimated closing bank balance at the end of the month. An overdrawn bank balance is shown in brackets.

timing problems with cash budgets

The main difficulty in the preparation of cash budgets lies in the timing of receipts and payments – for example, debtors (customers given credit terms) may pay two months after the date of sale, or suppliers may be paid one month after date of purchase: the information given in each case should be studied carefully to ensure that such receipts and payments are correctly recorded.

We now look at a practical example of a cash budget in the form of a Case Study.

CASE STUDY: COUNTRYCRAFT – THE CASH BUDGET

the business

Countrycraft is a manufacturer of traditional style pine furniture, its main product being kitchen tables. It is operated as a sole trader business by its owner Tim Chipping in a leased converted mill three miles outside Mereford. Tim runs a van in which he delivers his furniture. Countrycraft sells mainly on credit to furniture stores in the area, although it does sell some goods for cash from the premises. It is New Year and Tim plans to expand the business: he wants to buy some new machinery for £5,000 in March, and is hoping for a loan for this amount from the bank. He is putting in £2,000 of new capital himself in January to help support the expansion. Helped by his accountant he has drawn up a sales budget, a production budget and a cash budget to include in a business plan which he will submit to the bank.

the figures

The construction of a cash budget can be a complex operation, particularly when the timing element of cash receipts and payments is taken into account. Tim has talked through the figures with his accountant, and has produced the following information which he will use in the forecast (shown on page 59):

receipts

cash sales	Tim reckons on taking £500 a month from cash sales on the premises.
from debtors	Sales on credit are paid for two months after the issue of the invoice, thus sales of £2,000 invoiced in the previous November will be paid for in January. The other credit sales figures are

- December sales of £5,000 received in February
- January sales of £3,000 received in March
- February sales of £4,000 received in April
- March sales of £4,500 received in May
- April sales of £4,000 received in June

capital	Tim is introducing £2,000 of new capital in January.
loans	Tim is anticipating raising a bank loan of £5,000 in March.

payments

cash purchases

Tim's cash purchases (materials paid for straightaway) will be January £400, February £200, March £400, April £300, May £400, June £400.

credit purchases

Tim pays for purchases of timber two months after the month of invoice, ie he will pay for November purchases of £2,000 at the end of January. The other credit purchases figures are:
- December purchases of £2,500 paid for in February
- January purchases of £3,000 paid for in March
- February purchases of £2,000 paid for in April
- March purchases of £2,000 paid for in May
- April purchases of £1,000 paid for in June

capital items

Tim plans to buy new machinery for £5,000 in March.

wages

The wage bill comes to £500 per month.

rent/rates

The rental and business rates amount to £3,000 and are payable in March.

insurance

Comprehensive premises insurance of £550 is due in February.

electricity

Tim calculates a quarterly electricity bill of £240 will be due in March.

telephone

Tim calculates a quarterly telephone bill of £300 will be due in April.

VAT

Tim calculates that he will have to pay VAT of £500 in March and in June (this represents VAT collected from his sales of furniture less any VAT paid on his purchases and expenses).

vehicle expenses

Tim runs a delivery van for the business; he calculates that he will pay £50 a month in petrol, plus road tax of £125 in March and insurance of £300 in May.

stationery

Tim calculates stationery will cost him about £50 a month.

postages

Tim calculates postages will be £50 a month. In March (when his catalogue is mailed), it will be £200.

bank charges

These are likely to be £145, charged in March.

interest

The interest charges for bank borrowing on overdraft will be approximately £35 in March and £25 in June

loan repayments

It is anticipated that the first repayment of the bank loan (to include interest) will be £500 in June.

advertising

Tim calculates a cost of £50 per month, with an extra £825 for his catalogue in March (March payment: £875).

sundries

Tim calculates a cost of £50 per month for 'one-off' expenses.

bank position

When the figures have been entered in the appropriate columns (see page 59 opposite), the following totals should be calculated in the far right-hand column and the bank summary at the bottom:

- the totals for each category of receipt or expense in the far right-hand column (total up across each row)

- total receipts (A) for each month, and the far right-hand column, ie work down the columns

- total payments (B) for each month, and the far right-hand column, ie work down the columns

- the total of all the 'totals' (A) and (B) in the far right-hand column, as a cross check

- lastly, total payments (B) should be subtracted from total receipts (A) for each month and the figure entered in the row marked 'Net Cash Flow (A – B)'; a positive figure indicates that money has flowed into the business during the month, a negative figure (shown in brackets) indicates that money has flowed out of the business during the month

The bank position can now be calculated:

opening bank balance   Insert the bank balance at the beginning of January in the row marked 'Opening bank balance', ie £100 in Tim's case, a figure he will have obtained from his cash book.

closing bank balance   This is the total of 'Net Cash Flow (A – B)' and opening bank; in Tim's case this is £1,350 plus £100 = £1,450. This figure should then also be written in as February's 'Opening Bank Balance'. The process is then repeated for February, ie £1,500 plus £1,450 = £2,950 (which is then March's opening bank balance).

The bottom line of the cash budget shows the all-important figure of the closing bank balance (the expected balance at the end of each month). A figure in brackets indicates an overdraft – ie the business will be borrowing from the bank on its current account. In this case Tim will be borrowing on overdraft in March (£2,720), April (£1,570) and May (£20). At the end of June the bank account will be back in credit, at an estimated figure of £1,305.

Note:
The cash budget will normally be for twelve months' trading, but for the sake of clarity in the text only six months' figures are shown on the cash budget for Countrycraft (see the next page).

Cash budget

name.......... Countrycraft ....period .... January – June 19-9 ....

	January £	February £	March £	April £	May £	June £	TOTAL £
RECEIPTS							
Cash sales	500	500	500	500	500	500	3,000
From debtors	2,000	5,000	3,000	4,000	4,500	4,000	22,500
Capital	2,000						2,000
Loans			5,000				5,000
Interest							
TOTAL RECEIPTS (A)	4,500	5,500	8,500	4,500	5,000	4,500	32,500
PAYMENTS							
Cash purchases	400	200	400	300	400	400	2,100
Credit purchases	2,000	2,500	3,000	2,000	2,000	1,000	12,500
Capital items			5,000				5,000
Wages	500	500	500	500	500	500	3,000
Rent/Rates			3,000				3,000
Insurance		550					550
Electricity			240				240
Telephone				300			300
VAT			500			500	1,000
Vehicle expenses	50	50	175	50	350	50	725
Stationery	50	50	50	50	50	50	300
Postages	50	50	200	50	50	50	450
Bank charges			145				145
Interest charges			35			25	60
Loan repayments						500	500
Advertising	50	50	875	50	50	50	1125
Sundries	50	50	50	50	50	50	300
TOTAL PAYMENTS (B)	3,150	4,000	14,170	3,350	3,450	3,175	31,295
NET CASH FLOW (A-B)	1,350	1,500	(5,670)	1,150	1,550	1,325	1,205
OPENING BANK BALANCE	100	1,450	2,950	(2,720)	(1,570)	(20)	100
CLOSING BANK BALANCE	1,450	2,950	(2,720)	(1,570)	(20)	1305	1305

problems with cash budgets

limitations

While a cash budget is a very useful guide, it is only as good as the estimates on which it is based. A cash budget which is based on optimistic sales for the next six or twelve months will show an equally optimistic picture of the bank balance; a budget that looks too far into the future may prove to be inaccurate in later months. As with all budgets it is necessary to make comparisons between actual and budget figures: variances need to be investigated. Indeed, many cash budget and cash flow forms have columns for both projected and actual figures.

problems with incorrect forecasting

It must be appreciated that cash budgets are only informed estimates of what the cash position of a business may be over a given period. If a business seriously overestimates the inflow of cash, it could have serious problems when that cash does not materialise. The major problem is depletion of working capital. As you will have seen in your studies, working capital is the lifeblood of a business, being the excess of current assets (money in hand and due in the short-term) over current liabilities (debts which have to be paid in the short-term). In basic terms, the business will have cash flow problems and may become insolvent (bankrupt) – the definition of insolvency being the inability to pay debts as they fall due. A worst view scenario might run along the following lines:

- cash due from debtors does not come in – a major debtor may have become bankrupt

- there is pressure on the bank account as important creditors and wages have to be paid – the bank manager is distinctly unhappy as the overdraft rises above the limit set by the bank, even though the borrowing is secured by a charge (mortgage) over the business premises

- the bank refuses to pay a cheque to a major supplier to whom the business owes money – the supplier refuses to supply any further goods on which the business depends for its production

- the business is unable to fulfil some important orders, so sales income falls further

- employees find that their wages are not being paid

- the bank decides that it is unlikely to be repaid and so it appoints an Administrative Receiver under its mortgage

- the business is closed down by the Receiver and the premises sold off to repay the bank overdraft

- the employees lose their jobs and the owners their business

This is an extreme situation, although regrettably it is all too common. The point here is not that if you make a mistake with your cash budget you are likely to become bankrupt, but rather that an appreciation of the cash flow position is critical for the management of any business.

a solution – the computer spreadsheet

Often the managers of a business will wish to change the assumptions on which the cash budget is based by saying 'what if?' For example:

- what if sales decline by 20%?

- what if our business rates rise by 50%?

- what if we buy a new machine three months earlier than planned?

Each of these examples will change the cash budget substantially, and any two of the three, or all three together, is likely to have a considerable effect on a previously calculated budget, and may lead to an increased bank overdraft requirement.

To answer 'what if?' questions, the whole cash budget has to be re-worked on the basis of the new assumptions. The reason for this is that, as the estimates of receipts and payments change each month, so the estimated closing month-end bank balance changes. This is where a computer spreadsheet is ideal for the preparation of cash budgets: each change can be put in, and the computer can be used to re-work all the calculations. A printout can be taken of each assumption and then passed to the management for their consideration. On pages 60 to 62 we look at how a cash budget can be input into a computer spreadsheet, using Countrycraft as an example.

the cash budget on a computer spreadsheet

If you are unfamiliar with computer spreadsheets you are advised to familiarise yourself with a standard spreadsheet program before reading the next three pages. Consult your tutor if you are having difficulties in this area.

The calculations on a cash budget are not particularly difficult, but they do take a long time if you are tackling the task with only pen, paper and calculator. Imagine the situation if you finish the forecast and then find that you have to revise the sales figures: you will have to re-calculate the Total Receipts line, the Net Cash Flow line and all the bank balances.

The task is, of course, made simple when you have input the worksheet onto a computer spreadsheet program. You will be able to change any figure, and the computer will do all the recalculations automatically, for example:

- projections of different levels of sales – optimistic, realistic and pessimistic

- projections of different levels of expenditure

- the effect of buying an asset at different times

In each case you will be able to see the effect on the critical figure of the closing bank balance which indicates the amount of money the business may have to borrow.

On pages 61 and 62 we set out a six-month cash budget for Countrycraft based on the forecast illustrated on page 57. The second of the forecasts shows the effect of a 25% fall in receipts from debtors. Look at the effect on the bank account – the 'bottom line'. Note also the decrease in VAT payable as the level of sales falls.

how to complete the spreadsheet

- Row 1 includes the name of the business and the heading 'Cash Budget'

- Row 2 shows the period involved, eg January – June 19-3

- Rows 3, 11, 13, 14, 33, 34 and 36 are left blank to make the presentation clearer

- Column A is used for labels

- Columns B to G show the six months of the forecast

- Column H shows the totals

use of formulas in the spreadsheet – column C

Extensive use is made here of the addition of a range of cells. You will need to check your computer manual to find the formula to use. The formula used here is =Sum(C7:C11) where all the cells between C7 and C11 are added together. Column C is used below for illustrative purposes.

The formulas are as follows:

- Row 12 – Total Receipts   =Sum(C7:C11)

- Row 35 – Total Payments   =Sum(C16:C32)

- Row 37 – Net Cash Flow   =C12 - C35

- Row 38 – Opening Bank   =B39

    – ie the closing bank balance of the previous month. Note that B38 is a value cell into which is entered the opening bank balance for the period.

- Row 39 – Closing Bank   =C37+C38

- Column H – Total column

    Each row is totalled, eg cell H7 is =Sum(B7:G7). Column H is also totalled vertically, in the same way as the other columns, except that cell H38 is =B38 and cell H39 is =G39

- Row 29 – Interest

    This figure may be estimated and entered as a value, or can be approximated by formula. If interest for January is charged at the end of the month, the formula in cell B29 will be =(B39*K2/100)/12. K2 (column K row 2) is the reference of a value cell into which can be entered the current interest rate.

	A	B	C	D	E	F	G	H
1	Name of Business: Countrycraft							
2	Period: January - June 19-9							
3								
4		Jan	Feb	Mar	Apl	May	Jun	Total
5		£	£	£	£	£	£	£
6	RECEIPTS							
7	Cash sales	500	500	500	500	500	500	3000
8	Cash from debtors	2000	5000	3000	4000	4500	4000	22500
9	Capital	2000						2000
10	Loans			5000				5000
11	Interest							
12	TOTAL RECEIPTS	4500	5500	8500	4500	5000	4500	32500
13								
14								
15	PAYMENTS							
16	Cash purchases	400	200	400	300	400	400	2100
17	Credit purchases	2000	2500	3000	2000	2000	1000	12500
18	Capital items	0	0	5000	0	0	0	5000
19	Wages	500	500	500	500	500	500	3000
20	Rent/rates	0	0	3000	0	0	0	3000
21	Insurance	0	550	0	0	0	0	550
22	Electricity	0	0	240	0	0	0	240
23	Telephone	0	0	0	300	0	0	300
24	VAT	0	0	500	0	0	500	1000
25	Vehicle expenses	50	50	175	50	350	50	725
26	Stationery	50	50	50	50	50	50	300
27	Postages	50	50	200	50	50	50	450
28	Bank charges	0	0	145	0	0	0	145
29	Interest	0	0	35	0	0	25	60
30	Loan repayments	0	0	0	0	0	500	500
31	Advertising	50	50	875	50	50	50	1125
32	Sundries	50	50	50	50	50	50	300
33								
34								
35	TOTAL PAYMENTS	3150	4000	14170	3350	3450	3175	31295
36								
37	NET CASHFLOW	1350	1500	-5670	1150	1550	1325	1205
38	OPENING BANK	100	1450	2950	-2720	-1570	-20	100
39	CLOSING BANK	1450	2950	-2720	-1570	-20	1305	1305
40								
41								
42								

Fig. 4.1 Countrycraft's cash budget on a computer spreadsheet

	A	B	C	D	E	F	G	H
1	Name of Business: Countrycraft							
2	Period: January - June 19-9							
3								
4		Jan	Feb	Mar	Apl	May	Jun	Total
5		£	£	£	£	£	£	£
6	RECEIPTS							
7	Cash sales	500	500	500	500	500	500	3000
8	Cash from debtors	1500	3750	2250	3000	3375	3000	16875
9	Capital	2000						2000
10	Loans			5000				5000
11	Interest							
12	TOTAL RECEIPTS	4000	4250	7750	3500	3875	3500	26875
13								
14								
15	PAYMENTS							
16	Cash purchases	400	200	400	300	400	400	2100
17	Credit purchases	2000	2500	3000	2000	2000	1000	12500
18	Capital items	0	0	5000	0	0	0	5000
19	Wages	500	500	500	500	500	500	3000
20	Rent/rates	0	0	3000	0	0	0	3000
21	Insurance	0	550	0	0	0	0	550
22	Electricity	0	0	240	0	0	0	240
23	Telephone	0	0	0	300	0	0	300
24	VAT	0	0	400	0	0	400	800
25	Vehicle expenses	50	50	175	50	350	50	725
26	Stationery	50	50	50	50	50	50	300
27	Postages	50	50	200	50	50	50	450
28	Bank charges	0	0	145	0	0	0	145
29	Interest	0	0	50	0	0	100	150
30	Loan repayments	0	0	0	0	0	500	500
31	Advertising	50	50	875	50	50	50	1125
32	Sundries	50	50	50	50	50	50	300
33								
34								
35	TOTAL PAYMENTS	3150	4000	14085	3350	3450	3150	31185
36								
37	NET CASHFLOW	850	250	-6335	150	425	350	-4310
38	OPENING BANK	100	950	1200	-5135	-4985	-4560	100
39	CLOSING BANK	950	1200	-5135	-4985	-4560	-4210	-4210
40								
41								
42								

Fig. 4.2 Countrycraft's cash budget showing a 25% reduction in receipts from debtors

dealing with variances

We have seen when compiling the cash budget that the projected figures are only estimates. It is common for the forecast to present two columns for each month: the projected figures are entered in the left-hand column and the actual figures are entered next to them in the right-hand column. Thus the projected and actual figures can be directly compared. The differences betwen the projected and the actual figures are known as variances. As we saw in the last chapter, there are two types of variance:

- favourable (positive) variances – results are better than expected – commonly abbreviated to 'FAV'
- adverse (negative) variances – results are worse than expected – commonly abbreviated to 'ADV'

Sometimes the variances are not large or significant, in which case no action need be taken. Sometimes the variances can be substantial, in which case action needs to be taken, and particularly if the variances are adverse. As we have seen, businesses often use computer spreadsheet programs – as demonstrated on the previous three pages – to construct budgets by building in different variables, eg levels of sales.

Variances can include:

- a rise in sales income
- a fall in sales income
- a rise in costs
- a fall in costs

We will look further at the treatment of variances in Chapter 6.

---

chapter summary

- In a fully developed budgeting system, subsidiary budgets will contribute to the master budget which comprises a profit statement and a projected balance sheet.

- An important subsidiary budget is the cash budget, which shows amounts which are forecast to be received and spent (including VAT), and projects a monthly bank balance.

- Incorrect forecasting can lead to problems with a business' working capital position, to cash flow problems, and even to insolvency.

- Many businesses find a computer spreadsheet a useful method of calculating and presenting these forecasts. A spreadsheet will enable a business to appreciate the effect on cash flow of a fall in income (or a rise in costs).

- Cash budgets are only estimates, and it is normal to compare the actual figures against the projections. The differences between the two are known as variances, and appropriate action should be taken if the variances are significant.

STUDENT ACTIVITIES

4.1   Jane Merton is setting up a business selling perfume. She intends to rent a small shop in Stourminster for cash sales. The bulk of her sales, however, will be on credit to a network of agents she has already established in the area. The agents sell from door-to-door, and she allows them 30 days' credit.

As she will need financing she has been advised by her accountant to draw up a cash budget for the first six months of trading (January – June 19-9), which she can present to the bank, along with her business plan. The projected figures are as follows:

income – cash in

Cash sales	£1,000 per month
Receipts from debtors	£5,000 Jan - Mar; £6,000 April; £7,000 May and June
Capital introduced	£5,000 in January
Loan from father	£5,000 in March (no repayments or interest for a year)

payments – cash out

Purchases	£6,000 for cash in January – a 'one-off' payment £4,000 monthly for credit purchases (ie one month's credit received – first payment in February)
Wages	£750 per month
Rent and rates	£4,900 lease payment in January, business rates £100 per month (from January)
Insurance	£650 to be paid in January
Electricity	£240 quarterly (from March)
Telephone	£300 in April
VAT due	Jane estimates the first quarter's VAT payment (due in April) will be £1,400
Stationery & postages	£100 monthly
Bank	Charges of £150 and interest of £100, both in March
Advertising	£50 monthly

(a)   You are to draw up a cash budget for Jane Merton, using a computer spreadsheet (if available), for the period January to June 19-9. You should start with a nil bank balance.

(b)   Estimate the amount Jane will need to borrow from the bank.

4.2   Andrew Page is starting up a business consultancy, which will give advice to existing businesses and help new businesses to get started. He and his colleague Henry Hardy plan to operate from a small office in Mereford. They will bill their clients monthly, and will ask for payment within 28 days of the invoice date. As their consultancy is a 'service' business, they will not have 'purchases' of materials or stock; their main expense is their salary of £1,500 each monthly. Their projected income and expenses are as follows:

income – cash in

Receipts from clients	£4,000 February to April; £5,000 May; £7,000 June
Capital introduced	£10,000 in January

payments – cash out

Office equipment	£2,500 in January
Salary	£3,000 per month (ie £1,500 each)
Lease payment	£2,900 in January
Rates	£100 per month
Insurance	£650 in January
Electricity	£200 quarterly from March
Telephone	£400 in April
VAT	Estimate of £1,400 for first quarter (due in April)
Stationery	£100 per month
Postages	£50 per month
Bank	Estimate of £200 charges and £75 interest due in March
Vehicle expenses	£350 per month
Advertising	£1,500 for business launch in January, thereafter £100 per month

You are to draw up a cash budget for the first six months of trading (January to June 19-9), assuming a nil bank balance at the beginning of January.

5 The master budget

introduction

So far in this book we have seen how the subsidiary budgets are set up – the sales, production and staffing budgets, and in the last chapter the cash budget. In this chapter we turn to the final stage in the budget setting process: the master budget – also known as the operating budget – which will be explained largely by means of a Case Study. The master budget normally comprises two financial statements:

- *the **projected profit statement** (in technical terms the 'trading and profit and loss account') which tells the owners how much profit the business is likely to make over a twelve month period*
- *the **projected balance sheet** which will show the position of the business at the end of the twelve month period, ie the assets (items owned by the business), the liabilties (items owed) and the capital (the owners' investment)*

It is assumed that by this stage in your studies you are familiar with the layout of these financial statements. If you are not, or if your recollection is hazy, you should revise the area before reading this chapter.

subsidiary budgets and the master budget

In order that you can place the master budget in context with the other budgets, we reproduce in fig. 5.1 on the opposite page the diagram from Chapter 3 showing how the budgeting system works. You will see that the master budget is compiled from a combination of:

- *functional budgets* – for example the *staffing budget* which will give the wages and salaries figure for the the projected profit statement and the *purchases budget* which will provide the cost of sales figure (also in the profit statement)
- *departmental budgets* – the individual costs which will combine to produce the expenses figures on the projected profit statement
- the *cash budget* – the flows in and out of the bank account of the business (see Chapter 4) – this forecast is closely linked with the projected profit statement in the master budget, as we will see in the Case Study

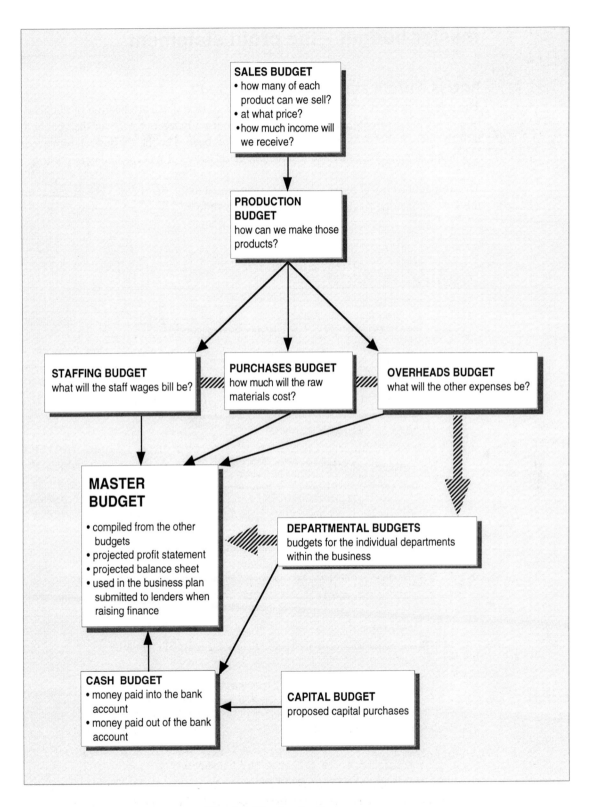

Fig. 5.1 The budgeting process

master budget – the profit statement

how is a profit statement constructed?

The profit statement usually covers a year of trading and is an indication of the level of activity and profitability of the business. It normally *looks back* over the year and tells the owner(s) how successful the business has been. The master budget, however, is a projection and *looks forward* to the budgeted levels of income and expenditure.

The format of a typical profit statement is illustrated in fig. 5.2 below. The business in this case is one that buys and sells goods – eg a shop.

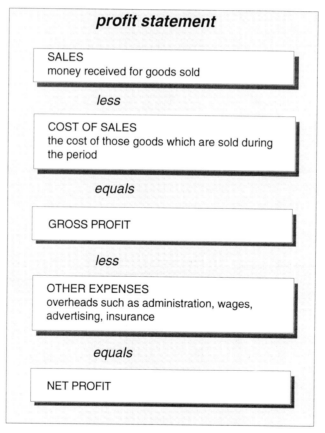

Fig. 5.2 The format of a profit statement

We will now explain:

- the terms used in the profit statement

- the sources of the figures used in the projected profit statement

sales

This is a record of the money amounts received (or due to be received) for goods sold, or services provided. The figure for the master budget will be taken from the *sales budget*.

cost of sales

In basic terms, cost of sales is what you have paid (or are due to pay) for what you have sold. It is calculated by adjusting the total of purchases for the year for any change in stock level if goods are involved (the calculation is: opening stock *plus* purchases *less* closing stock). Effectively you are saying that what you have sold is:

> *stock in the warehouse at the beginning of the year*
> *plus*
> *stock you have bought during the year*
> *less*
> *stock left in the warehouse at the end of the year*

The source of the figures for the master budget is the *purchases budget*.

gross profit

Gross profit is trading profit, ie profit before any dedutions are made for overhead expenses. It is common to express gross profit as a percentage of sales; the formula for this is:

$$\frac{gross\ profit \times 100}{sales} \quad = \quad gross\ profit\ percentage$$

other expenses

These expenses – often called *overheads* – include items such as wages, rent and rates, services (electricity and telephone), vehicle expenses, financial costs, advertising, insurance and depreciation. These figures will be taken from the *functional budgets* (eg staffing) and/or the *departmental budgets*.

Note that *depreciation* is the cost to the business of the wear and tear of assets owned, eg the fall in value of cars and computers over time. It is an expense to the business which does not involve cash, although, of course, at the end of the day the assets will probably have to be replaced. The depreciation figures for each year will be deducted from the profit in the profit statement and also from the value of the assets in the balance sheet. Larger businesses will set up a *depreciation budget* to calculate the appropriate figures.

net profit

Net profit is the final profit after deduction of all expenses which will be due to the owner(s) of the business, hence the expression: "the bottom line". Net profit is often expressed as a percentage of sales to provide an indicator of the profitability of a business. The formula is:

$$\frac{net\ profit \times 100}{sales} \quad = \quad net\ profit\ percentage$$

preparing the the profit forecast

preparing figures for the profit forecast

On the next page is illustrated a profit forecast for an existing business, Osborne Electronics Limited. Notes explaining how the figures are derived are set out below. For the sake of clarity, only six months' figures are shown, rather than the usual twelve months' figures. Following the illustration is a Case Study showing how a business draws up a cash budget, a projected profit statement, and then extracts a projected balance sheet from these figures.

definition

A profit forecast is a budgeted projection of expected sales, expected costs and expected profit on a monthly basis over a specific period of time – here six months. Because sales and purchases are made on credit (they are paid for later) the forecast shows the *profit* position rather than the *cash* position (bank account) of the business.

time period

The time period shown is normally twelve months; as noted above, six months' figures are shown here for the sake of clarity. The vertical columns show the figures for each month with a total figure for the time period on the right.

sales

Sales is the invoiced value of the sales during the month. It is *not* the amount of money received for sales during the month. This figure does not include VAT (where the business is registered for VAT).

cost of sales

Cost of sales is the cost of what has been sold during the month. The figure is normally based on the purchases figure, adjusted for opening and closing stock (add opening stock, deduct closing stock). This figure does not include VAT (where the business is registered for VAT).

expenses

The figures entered in the expenses section represent the monthly cost of the expenses incurred, whether or not the bills have actually been paid. You will see from the example that some items, electricity for example, are averaged out over the six month period, even if they are paid for quarterly. VAT is not included in the expenses figures (where the business is registered for VAT).

total expenses

The total expenses figure is the total of all the items below the gross profit calculation. It must be stressed again that this figure does not represent cash paid out – it is the total of the expenses incurred during the month, and in all probability paid for later.

net profit

Forecast net profit is calculated by deducting total expenses from gross profit. If expected net profit is negative – ie a *loss* is made – the figure is commonly shown in brackets.

Profit statement forecast

name..........Osborne Electronics Limited..........period..........January – June 19-9..........

	January £	February £	March £	April £	May £	June £	TOTAL £
Sales	5,000	5,000	6,000	5,000	5,000	5,000	31,000
Less: Cost of Sales	2,500	2,500	3,500	2,500	2,500	2,500	16,000
Gross Profit	2,500	2,500	2,500	2,500	2,500	2,500	15,000
Gross Profit %	50	50	42	50	50	50	48
Expenses							
Wages	500	500	500	500	500	500	3,000
Rent/Rates	150	150	150	150	150	150	900
Insurance	40	40	40	40	40	40	240
Electricity	25	25	25	25	25	25	150
Telephone	35	35	35	35	35	35	210
Other services	55	55	55	55	55	55	330
Vehicle expenses	50	50	50	50	50	50	300
Stationery	10	10	10	10	10	10	60
Postages	55	55	55	55	55	55	330
Bank charges							
Interest charges							
Professional fees						100	100
Advertising	50	50	50	50	50	50	300
Sundries	35	35	35	35	35	35	210
Depreciation	100	100	100	100	100	100	600
Total Expenses	1,105	1,105	1,105	1,105	1,105	1,205	6,730
Net Profit/ (Loss)	1,395	1,395	1,395	1,395	1,395	1,295	8,270

CASE STUDY
IAN PHILLIPS – DRAWING UP THE MASTER BUDGET

Ian Phillips is an expert in computer software. He has worked until recently for a leading British software house which made him redundant four months ago. He has £10,000 available from his redundancy money and savings to invest as capital, and wishes to set up a computer software shop in a new shopping arcade, which is offering units at preferential rates. He has named his venture 'Software Stores'. It will open on 1 January 19-9.

His customers will include the general public and also local businesses who need expert guidance on the setting up of business packages.

He wishes to raise finance from the bank but is not sure how much he needs. On a friend's recommendation he has approached Jim Stoner, a local accountant, who is known to specialise in small business finance. Jim has been helping Ian draw up a business plan.

Ian has now got to the stage where he can draw up the master budget. Jim gathers the following information from his client:

income

■ Ian Phillips has capital of £10,000 in the building society; he wants to invest this into the business

■ expected cash sales from callers at the shop are £3,000 per month

■ expected credit sales from business software are £1,000 per month on 60 days' credit (ie sales made in January will be paid for in March)

expenditure

■ purchase of stock of £5,000 in January is to be paid for immediately by cheque (stock will be reduced to a level of £3,250 at the end of each month, following estimated sales of £1,750 [at cost] of stock each month); the 'closing stock' figure for the profit forecast (and for the balance sheet) will therefore be £3,250

■ after January stock purchases by Ian will be £1,750 each month:

(a)   in February and March paid for immediately by cheque

(b)   from April onwards, all purchases on 30 days' credit (eg April's purchases will be paid for in the month following purchase, ie in May)

The reason for (a) and (b) is that credit will often only be granted by suppliers after the business has shown that it is creditworthy, usually after a few months' trading.

■ equipment purchases (fixed assets) £4,500, to be paid for in January

■ the telephone, bought in January will cost £135 (a fixed asset); the monthly running cost will be £15

■ Ian buys shop fixtures and fittings (fixed assets) £5,250, to be paid for in February

■ monthly payments the business will make are:
  • rent and rates £575
  • insurance £50
  • electricity £25
  • stationery £10
  • postages £15
  • drawings (ie Ian taking money out of the business) £750

■ advertising will cost £150 in January and £30 in subsequent months

■ bank charges: arrangement fee of £100 and quarterly charges of £75 in March and June

■ Ian estimates that bank overdraft interest of £65 will be payable in March

■ six months' depreciation of fixed assets is to be charged (in the profit and loss account) at £750 (£125 per month); the separate amounts for depreciation are office equipment £350, fixtures and fittings £400

NOTE: as depreciation is a non-cash item it does not appear in the cash budget.

processing of the figures

Jim helps Ian to draw up a cash budget and a forecast profit statement (illustrated on the following pages). Jim recommends that Ian does not register for VAT until the level of sales justifies it. The appropriate figures therefore include VAT.

cash budgets and profit forecasts compared

Note from this Case Study that the drawing up of the cash budget is an integral part of the processing of the master budget – the two budgets use the same information and have much in common. It must be remembered, however, that:

• the cash budget includes VAT; the profit forecast for a VAT registered business does not

• the cash budget shows the flow of money as it passes through the bank account; the profit forecast shows when the income and expenditure is incurred – this is not the same thing: businesses often buy and sell goods and then make payment (or receive payment) two months later

• the cash budget covers all items of income and expenditure, including the receipt of loans and the purchase of fixed assets, the profit forecast does not include these items.

completion of the profit forecast

sales
Total monthly sales of £4,000 comprise cash sales of £3,000 and invoiced credit sales of £1,000. Note that these figures represent sales as they are made and not – in the case of credit sales – the money that is received.

cost of sales
The monthly cost of sales is the cost of the stock actually sold, here £1,750 per month. The formula is:

cost of sales = opening stock + purchases – closing stock

The calculation for January is therefore

cost of sales = 0 + £5,000 – £3,750 = £1,750

The calculation for February and subsequent months is

cost of sales = £3,750 + £1,750 – £3,750 = £1,750

Remember that closing stock for one month is the opening stock for the following month.

gross profit
This figure is the difference between sales and cost of sales. Sometimes (as here) a profit and loss forecast will show the gross profit percentage.

wages
There is no entry here because Ian's drawings do not feature in the profit and loss account, but are deducted in the capital section of the balance sheet (see below).

expenses
The expenses are generally averaged out over the six month period and allocated to each month.

telephone
The cost of £135 becomes a fixed asset and only the running costs (£15 per month) are shown in the profit and loss account. The cost of the machine is a capital item which will appear in the cash flow forecast (cash spent) and in the balance sheet (see below). The purchase price of capital items cannot be set off against profit.

interest
The estimated bank account interest is shown in the March column as it is a charge for the January – March quarter.

depreciation
The depreciation – wear and tear on the assets – is shown as a monthly charge of £125. Note that this will never appear in the cash flow forecast, as it is not a cash expense, but an indication in the accounts of the fall in value of an asset, and therefore an expense to the business.

net profit
Net profit is calculated as

gross profit less total expenses

Net profit is the profit due to the owner of the business. It is, of course, subject to tax, which in the case of Ian Phillips will be charged in an income tax assessment issued by the Inland Revenue. It is also available for drawings (money taken out of the business by the owner), an item which appears in the cash budget but not in the profit and loss forecast.

Profit statement forecast

name.......Software Stores...period January – June 19-9.

	January £	February £	March £	April £	May £	June £	TOTAL £
Sales	4,000	4,000	4,000	4,000	4,000	4,000	24,000
Less: Cost of Sales	1,750	1,750	1,750	1,750	1,750	1,750	10,500
Gross Profit	2,250	2,250	2,250	2,250	2,250	2,250	13,500
Gross Profit %	56	56	56	56	56	56	56
Expenses							
Wages							
Rent/Rates	575	575	575	575	575	575	3,450
Insurance	50	50	50	50	50	50	300
Electricity	25	25	25	25	25	25	150
Telephone	15	15	15	15	15	15	90
Other services							
Vehicle expenses							
Stationery	10	10	10	10	10	10	60
Postages	15	15	15	15	15	15	90
Bank charges	100		75			75	250
Interest charges			65				65
Professional fees							
Advertising	150	30	30	30	30	30	300
Sundries							
Depreciation	125	125	125	125	125	125	750
Total Expenses	1,065	845	985	845	845	920	5,505
Net Profit (Loss)	1,185	1,405	1,265	1,405	1,405	1,330	7,995

Cash budget

name.. Software Stores .... period. January – June 19–9

	January £	February £	March £	April £	May £	June £	TOTAL £
RECEIPTS							
Cash sales	3,000	3,000	3,000	3,000	3,000	3,000	18,000
Cash from debtors			1,000	1,000	1,000	1,000	4,000
Capital	10,000						10,000
Loans							
TOTAL RECEIPTS (A)	13,000	3,000	4,000	4,000	4,000	4,000	32,000
PAYMENTS							
Cash purchases	5,000	1,750	1,750				8,500
Credit purchases					1,750	1,750	3,500
Capital items	4,635	5,250					9,885
Wages							
Rent/Rates	575	575	575	575	575	575	3,450
Insurance	50	50	50	50	50	50	300
Electricity	25	25	25	25	25	25	150
Telephone	15	15	15	15	15	15	90
VAT							
Vehicle expenses							
Stationery	10	10	10	10	10	10	60
Postages	15	15	15	15	15	15	90
Bank charges	100		75			75	250
Interest charges			65				65
Professional fees							
Advertising	150	30	30	30	30	30	300
Drawings	750	750	750	750	750	750	4,500
TOTAL PAYMENTS (B)	11,325	8,470	3,360	1,470	3,220	3,295	31,140
NET CASHFLOW (A-B)	1,675	(5,470)	640	2,530	780	705	860
OPENING BANK BALANCE	0	1,675	(3,795)	(3,155)	(625)	155	0
CLOSING BANK BALANCE	1,675	(3,795)	(3,155)	(625)	155	860	860

completion of the balance sheet ───────────────

Jim now shows Ian the source of all the figures for the forecast balance sheet, the final part of the master budget.

It is assumed at this point that you are familiar with the format of a balance sheet. Refer to the completed balance sheet on the next page, and if you do not understand the layout, consult your tutor or main textbook (for example Osborne Books' *Business Studies*, Chapter 36).

item	*source*	*details*
fixed assets	*cash budget*	office equipment of £4,635 (including the telephone costing £135) and shop fixtures and fittings, recorded in January and February respectively
depreciation	*profit forecast*	depreciation (abbreviated to 'Dep'n') is the last expense item in the profit forecast – the split between £400 and £350 has been supplied by Ian Phillips
stock	*profit forecast*	stock in the current assets section is always the closing stock figure from the cost of sales calculation
debtors	*profit forecast*	debtors is the total of credit sales not yet paid for: in this case, two months' sales £1,000 plus £1,000 = £2,000
bank	*cash budget*	bank in the current assets section is the closing bank balance from the cash budget (bottom right-hand figure); a negative figure – an overdraft – would be recorded as a current liability
creditors	*profit forecast*	this figure represents one month's purchases not yet paid for (ie the cost of sales £1,750); note that if the business had been given two months' credit, the figure would be doubled
capital	*cash budget*	£10,000 is introduced in January (receipts section)
net profit	*profit forecast*	the bottom right-hand figure from the profit forecast – the total net profit for the period
drawings	*cash budget*	the last expense item in the cash budget

The completed balance sheet is set out on the next page.

IAN PHILLIPS TRADING AS SOFTWARE STORES
FORECAST BALANCE SHEET AS AT 30 JUNE 19-9

	Cost	Dep'n	Net
	£	£	£
Fixed Assets			
Office equipment	4,635	350	4,285
Fixtures and fittings	5,250	400	4,850
	9,885	750	9,135
Current Assets			
Stock		3,250	
Debtors		2,000	
Bank		860	
		6,110	
Less Current Liabilities			
Creditors		1,750	
Working Capital			4,360
NET ASSETS			13,495
FINANCED BY			
Capital			10,000
Add net profit			7,995
			17,995
Less drawings			4,500
			13,495

how the master budget is used

The master budget is useful to the business in a number of ways:

monitoring

The forecast profit statement will be monitored, often on a monthly basis. Reports will be produced and the actual results compared with the budgeted figures. Variances will be detected, and action taken where appropriate or possible. This subject will be explained in more detail in the next chapter. For our purposes here it is enough to note that the master budget enables the owner(s) of the business to see how the business is progressing in all aspects – sales, costs and expenses. Without the benefit of the master budget the business could be running into problems of which the owner(s) could be quite unaware.

the 'business plan' for a lender

The master budget, together with the cash budget, form the basis of the financial section of the business plan – the document which will be prepared by the business when it wishes to raise money from a lender or investing company. You will probably already have studied – and maybe even written – a business plan as part of your coursework. You will know that the financial element of the plan is central to the case which the business will present to, say, the bank. A business may have an excellent product and a growing market share, but without financial projections to back up its other forecasts, it will not be able to convince anyone to lend their money.

chapter summary

■ The master budget is compiled from the subsidiary budgets of a business.

■ The master budget comprises
  • a profit statement
  • a forecast balance sheet

■ The master budget is normally compiled in conjunction with the cash budget.

■ The master budget enables the owner(s) of the business to plan effectively – normally over twelve months – and to monitor the success (or otherwise) of the business.

■ The master budget, together with the cash budget, form the basis of the financial section of the business plan which will be presented to a potential lender or investor when the business wants to raise money,

STUDENT ACTIVITIES

5.1   The accountant of Wilkinson Ltd. is preparing the company's cash budget for the first six months of 19-7. The following budgeted figures are available:

	Sales	Purchases	Wages and salaries	Other expenses
	£	£	£	£
January	65,000	26,500	17,500	15,500
February	70,000	45,000	18,000	20,500
March	72,500	50,000	18,250	19,000
April	85,000	34,500	18,500	18,500
May	65,000	35,500	16,500	20,500
June	107,500	40,500	20,000	22,000

The following additional information is available:

- Sales income is received in the month after sale, and sales for December 19-6 amounted to £57,500.
- 'Other expenses' each month includes an allocation of £1,000 for depreciation; all other expenses are paid for in the month in which they are incurred.
- Purchases, and wages and salaries are paid for in the month in which they are incurred.
- The bank balance at 1 January 19-7 is £2,250.
- Stock at 1 January 19-7 is valued at £15,500 and, at 30 June 19-7, is expected to have a value of £17,350.

You are to prepare:

(a)   a month-by-month cash budget for the first six months of 19-7

(b)   a budgeted profit statement for the six months ending 30 June 19-7

5.2 Jim Smith has recently been made redundant; he has received a redundancy payment and this, together with his accumulated savings, amounts to £10,000. He has decided to set up his own business selling computer stationery and this will commence trading with an initial capital of £10,000 on 1 January. On this date he will buy a van for business use at a cost of £6,000. He has estimated his purchases, sales, and expenses for the next six months as follows:

	Purchases	Sales	Expenses
	£	£	£
January	4,500	1,250	750
February	4,500	3,000	600
March	3,500	4,000	600
April	3,500	4,000	650
May	3,500	4,500	650
June	4,000	6,000	700

He will pay for purchases in the month after purchase; likewise, he expects his customers to pay for sales in the month after sale. All expenses will be paid for in the month in which they are incurred.

Jim realizes that he may need bank overdraft facilities before his business becomes established. He asks you to help him with information for the bank and, in particular, he asks you to prepare:

(a) a month-by-month cash budget for the first six months

(b) a forecast profit statement for the first six months – for this he tells you that his closing stock at 30 June is expected to have a value of £3,250, and that he wishes to depreciate the van at 20% per annum

(c) a budgeted balance sheet as at 30 June

5.3 Peter Sanderson has worked for some years as a sales representative for an arts and craft company, but has recently been made redundant. He intends to start up in business in October on his own, using £15,000 which he currently has invested with a building society. He has a number of good business contacts, and is confident that his firm will do well, but thinks that additional finance will be required in the short term; he plans to approach his bank for the necessary finance. Peter, whom you have known for some time, asks you for advice. The current year is 19-3.

He provides the following information:

- Arrangements have been made to purchase fixed assets costing £8,000. These will be paid for at the end of September and are expected to have a five year life, at the end of which they will have a nil scrap value.

- Stocks costing £5 000 will be bought and paid for on 28 September, and subsequent monthly purchases will be at a level sufficient to replace forecast sales for the month.

- Forecast monthly sales are £3,000 for October, £6,000 for November and December, and £10,500 from January 19-4 onwards.

- Selling price is fixed at the cost of stock plus 50%.

- Two months' credit will be allowed to customers, but only one month's credit will be received from suppliers of stock (but the initial stock will be paid for immediately).

- Running expenses, including rent but excluding depreciation of fixed assets, are estimated at £1,600 per month.

- Peter intends to make monthly cash drawings from the bank of £1,000.

You are to prepare:

(a) A month-by-month cash budget for the six months to 31 March 19-4.

(b) A budgeted profit statement for the six months to 31 March 19-4, and a forecast balance sheet as at 31 March 19-4.

(c) An assessment of his forecasts and financial requirements from a lender's (ie bank's) viewpoint.

5.4 You are planning to set up in business at the beginning of the year 19-8. Your enterprise is a small bookshop which you will call 'Anne's Bookshop'.

You plan to introduce capital of £6,000 in January. You also intend to purchase for cash an initial stock of books costing £5,000, together with fixtures and fittings costing £3,750, also to be paid for in January. You hope to start trading in January 19-8 and you have estimated sales for the first six months as follows:

January	£3,000
February	£2,400
March	£3,600
April	£4,500
May	£4,200
June	£3,900

All sales will be for cash. You plan to work to a gross profit margin of one-third of the selling price (ie in January the cost price of books sold for £30,000 will be £20,000). Towards the end of each month you will replenish the stock to ensure that, at the month-end, it will be restored to £5,000. Your suppliers for book purchases, excluding the initial cash stock purchase, will allow one month's credit (eg purchases made in January will be paid for in February).

You estimate the monthly overheads of the shop will be:

rent and rates	£250
wages	£280
heat/light/telephone	£95

You plan to withdraw from the bank for your own use drawings of £500 per month. Your accountant has advised you to depreciate fixtures and fittings at the rate of 20% per annum (straight line method). Interest costs are to be ignored.

Your accountant also advises you to prepare, for the six months ending 30 June 19-8:

- a cash budget (using a spreadsheet if it is available)
- a profit forecast
- a forecast balance sheet as at 30 June 19-8

These documents will form part of the Business Plan which you will submit to the bank as part of your application for the finance, which your accountant suspects you will need. Prepare the documents and pass them to your accountant for checking.

6 Budget monitoring

introduction

In the last three chapters we have looked at the way budgets are set up and how the subsidiary budgets contribute to the cash budget and the master budget. In this chapter we examine the control systems that are set up in a business to monitor the budgets – to see how well the planned peformance targets are met, and if they are not, to find out why, so that action can be taken as necessary. We will look at:

- *the control systems within a business*
- *how budget 'variances' are reported within the business*
- *how budgets can be 'flexible' to changes in circumstances*

budget planning and control

budget planning

As we have seen in earlier chapters, the planning of a budget is normally co-ordinated by the *budget co-ordinator* – a member of the accounts or finance department of a business. Many larger organisations take a highly formal view of planning the budgets and, as we saw in Chapter 2, form a budget committee. The left-hand column of fig. 6.1 opposite shows a diagrammatic approach to budget (or 'budgetary') planning.

budgetary control

Once a budget has been approved by the owner, senior management, or board of directors it becomes the official plan of the business for the period of the budget. There is no point in a business spending a lot of time and effort in preparing a budget if it is not used as a control mechanism throughout the period: this function is known as *budgetary control.*

The main aspect with which budgetary control is concerned is in comparing actual results with what was planned to happen in the budget. Fig. 6.1 also shows how budgetary control should be used to provide information both to those who are responsible for managing budgets and to the owner or board of directors.

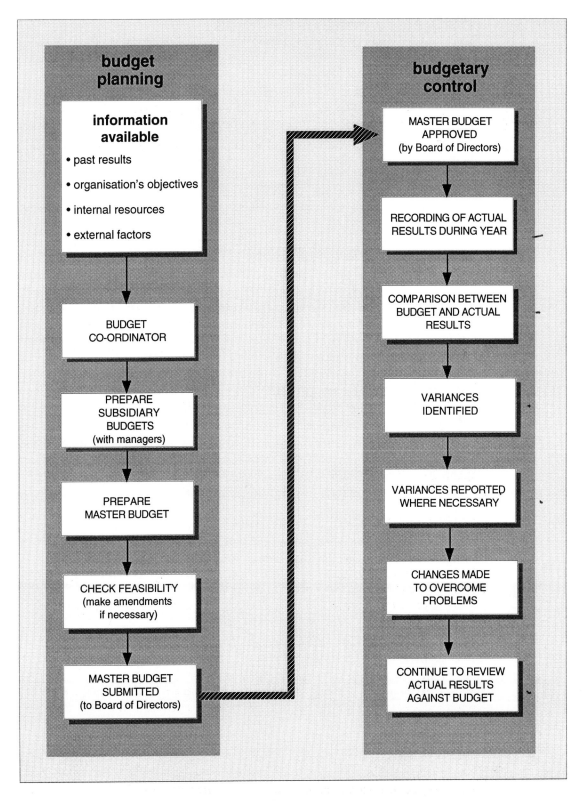

Fig. 6.1 Budgetary planning and control

budgetary control systems

responsibility for budgets

The setting of budgets for different departments – the budget centres – within an organisation implies that an individual – normally the departmental manager – is *personally responsible* for the budget as *budget holder*. He or she will see to it that the various targets are met. These targets might include costs (for a production department) or income (for a sales department). This accountability for budgets is what is known as *responsibility accounting*. This responsibility should *motivate* the manager and the supervisors to achieve the required level of performance. Some businesses give managers and supervisors incentives and bonuses for meeting targets, or improving upon them.

monitoring results – variances

The budget, once it is set for the financial year, is monitored by comparing actual results with the targeted figures. Any differences between the two are known as *variances*. This is all very well, but the question should then be asked – when is a variance *significant*? A variance of £1,000 in one month – for example an overrun in raw material costs – may be critical in a small business, but to a large car manufacturer it may be of less significance.

management by exception

It is essential, therefore, that the budgetary control system of a business will set down procedures for *acting on* variances, but only variances that matter. This type of system is known as *management by exception*, ie acting on variances that are exceptional. What is exceptional? Departmental managers will normally work on *control limits* imposed on costs. A control limit is an acceptable percentage variation on the budgeted cost. If the cost exceeds the control limit, the variance will be significant and investigative action will need to be taken. For example the labour cost for a production department may be budgeted at £50,000 a month, with a control limit of 5% set. If labour costs in any one month exceed £50,000 x 5%, ie a variance of £2,500, action will have to be taken and the cause investigated. Look at fig. 6.2 below.

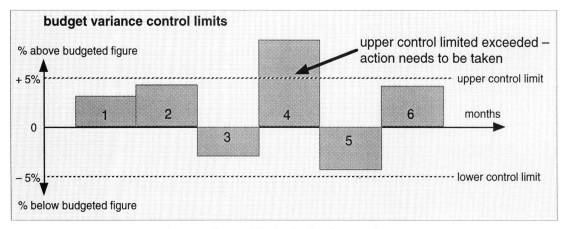

Fig. 6.2 Control limits for budget variances

who needs to know about variances?

In Chapter 2 we examined the financial management of a business. You will recall that many business organisations have *hierarchical* structures – the operations and management of the business are carried out by staff in a series of *levels*, ranging in a limited company from the managing director at the top, the other directors, departmental managers and supervisors to the production and administrative staff.

Variances in budgets need to be reported to the *appropriate* level in the hierarchy (management levels). The level of management involved will depend on the significance of the variance, as shown in the two extreme examples which follow:

Example 1

The sales department office has spent £50 over budget on stationery.

The managing director is unlikely to be interested – it will be up to the office supervisor to sort out the problem.

Example 2

Sales of one product exceed the sales budget by 50% – a runaway success!

This is a matter to bring to the attention of higher management and board level of the company: production patterns, purchasing and staffing will have to be re-organised so that production of that item can be increased.

Fig 6.3 below sets out the areas of responsibility for variances in *labour* cost.

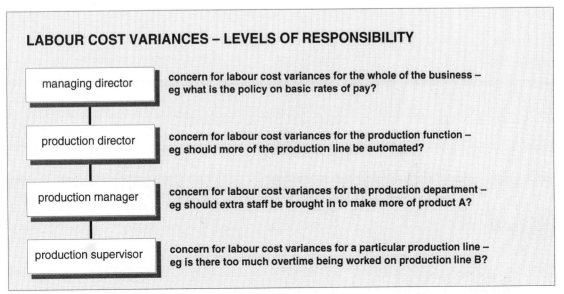

Fig. 6.3 Variances and levels of responsibility

reporting variances

Departmental managers in a business (in charge of 'budget centres') will base their decisions on departmental budget reports which present:

budgeted figures <u>less</u> actual figures = variances

These budget reports are likely to be produced on a computer printout by the finance department and circulated to departmental mangers for comment and action. The reports will be very detailed and list every item of expenditure and income. The items will often be identified by computer code. Less significant variances will be dealt with by the manager and his supervisors; significant variances will need to be referred to a higher management level. Many variances will not need reporting: the overspending on stationery mentioned on the previous page being an example. Summarised reports – including the master budget – will be circulated to higher management to provide a picture of how the business is meeting its targets.

Fig 6.4 below sets out the format of a typical budget report for a sales department. Note that the illustration shows only an extract from the report; in reality many more products would be shown, and possibly also a breakdown of sales by area and sales reprentative. The details shown are:

- the budget centre (sales department) and the budget holder (manager) responsible
- budget, actual and variance figures for the current period (here June)
- year-to-date figures
- the variance trend: 'FAV' is short for 'favourable' ie better than budget, 'ADV' is short for 'adverse' ie worse than budget
- comments – the column here would suffice for simple reasons,but the manager would expect to receive a more detailed report for significant variances

BUDGETARY CONTROL REPORT

budget centre Sales Dept   date 07.11.19-5

budget holder R Brunson   period October 19-5

	current period			Year-to-date			trend	comments
	budget £000s	actual £000s	variance £000s	budget £000s	actual £000s	variance £000s		
PRODUCT A	200	250	+ 50	2,750	3,125	+ 375	FAV	
PRODUCT B	225	200	– 25	1,275	1,150	– 125	ADV	
PRODUCT C	425	450	+ 25	4,025	4,475	+ 450	FAV	
etc ...								

Fig. 6.4 Format of a budget report (extract only)

investigating variances

changes in income

The sale of goods and services provides the main income for most businesses. It comprises the number of items sold, or units of service provided, multiplied by the price of the item. The sales income will therefore vary according to the number of items sold and the price charged.

A rise in sales income is clearly desirable, as shown in the report illustrated on the previous page. If a business has a number of different products, the successful items should be identified and efforts made to increase sales of them further.

A fall in sales income might be brought about by:

- *overpricing* – if the item is priced too highly when compared with the competition, the price may need to be reduced to stimulate demand
- *price-cutting* – this is sometimes necessary when there is a lot of competition amongst providers, eg supermarkets, garages
- *slack consumer demand* – if the level of spending in the economy is low, or interest rates are high, consumer demand could be stimulated by 'special offers'

changes in expenditure

Expenditure costs comprise:

- purchase of goods which are going to be sold (eg for a shop)
- purchase of materials for a manufacturing business
- costs for the administration of the business, eg staff, equipment, consumables, etc

A *fall* in costs is generally considered to be an acceptable variance (although sales income may also have fallen).

A *rise* in costs can arise from a number of factors:

- a rise caused by a general price rise, or by buying from a different supplier, or in smaller (more expensive) quantities
- a rise in the cost of imported items following exchange rate fluctuations, eg Japanese electronic goods will cost more in Britain if the pound falls against the Japanese Yen

Note also that one cost in a budget may increase, but will lead to a reduction in another cost. For example, a switch from a manual to a computer accounting system will increase the equipment and expenses budget heads (new computers and software have to be purchased), but should reduce the staff budget heads for the accounts department (as fewer staff will be needed).

Variances and their causes are discussed further in Chapter 9.

timing the budget reports

The timescale of the report will depend on the budget periods used. For example, if the budget has been prepared on the basis of budget periods of a month, then budget variations are likely to be reported within the first two weeks of the next budget period – often in the form of a computer printout from the finance department. Generally a manager will call a meeting at a fixed point in a budget period to review budget variations from the previous budget period with the staff responsible for the budget. This date establishes the timescale of the reporting, for example:

WEEK 1

all income and expenditure from the *previous* budget
period must have been produced by the beginning of week 2

WEEK 2

actual figures from the previous budget period must be analysed
by the end of week 2 so that the budget report can be completed

---

WEEK 3

the budget review meeting can then be held at the beginning of
week 3 of each budget period

---

fixed and flexible budgets

fixed budgets

a fixed budget remains the same whatever the level of output of the business

So far in this book we have taken a simple view of budget setting. We have assumed that budgets have been set at the beginning of the financial year and then adhered to and monitored, whatever the circumstances – ie the budgeted figures do not change. This is the *fixed budget*. This type of budget will be useful in situations where circumstances are stable – for example a departmental budget for a school or a college, where a set amount of money is set aside for buying textbooks each year.

flexible budgets

In commercial situations, however, situations do change. For example, the sale of products can vary widely from the target figures in the budget: a new product can be more successful than expected – or it can be a complete disaster. In either case the budgeted figures for sales (and production costs too) will be wide of the mark. The answer is to use a *flexible budget*. A flexible budget will vary in line with the level of output of a business – ie with the number of products sold or services provided:

a flexible budget is a <u>series of budgets</u> for the same budget period showing figures for a range of levels of output

A business may therefore prepare a flexible production budget assuming 100%, 90%, 80% and 70% of normal output. If production is at 80% of capacity, the budget is 'flexed' so that the 80% option can be used, and appropriate variances calculated.

flexible budgets – fixed and variable costs

When calculating costs for a flexible budget, certain costs vary with the level of output, eg

* materials costs for a manufacturing business
* direct labour costs – the production line workforce wages bill

The other costs of making a product (or providing a service), eg office rent, warehouse rent, fuel bills, insurance, office staff wages – the *overheads* – fall into two categories:

* fixed overheads, eg the rent of an office
* variable overheads, eg sales commission

The important point here is that when constructing a flexible budget, fixed overheads will normally remain the same, whatever the level of output, but variable overheads will change in line with the percentage of output.

CASE STUDY
PITMAN PLASTICS – FIXED AND FLEXIBLE BUDGETS

situation
Pitman Plastics manufactures plastic kitchenware. The production manager has just extracted the cost figures for last month's output and is comparing them with the budgeted figures:

	budget	actual
	£	£
materials cost	100,000	81,000
labour cost	50,000	42,000
overheads	50,000	44,000
TOTAL	200,000	167,000

The results, on the face of it, look very encouraging – costs are £33,000 below budget. The manager knows, however, that sales have been depressed during the month and also that production has been running at 80% of normal capacity. Would it make any difference to the results if the finance department produced a flexible budget – at 80% of output? They agree to do so, noting that at 100% production the overheads are split equally between fixed and variable categories.

solution

The fixed budget report based on the figures given shows an overall (total) <u>favourable</u> variance of costs, being £33,000 below budget. The production director knows that this is misleading.

fixed budget report

	budget	actual	variance	trend
output level	100%			
	£	£	£	
materials cost	100,000	81,000	19,000	FAV
labour cost	50,000	42,000	8,000	FAV
overheads	50,000	44,000	6,000	FAV
TOTAL	200,000	167,000	33,000	FAV

The flexible budget report, based on costs for 80% output shows an overall (total) <u>adverse</u> variance of £2,000. This is a more realistic picture of performance, and is less encouraging. Note that while fixed overhead costs remain at £25,000 for 80% production, budgeted variable overheads have been reduced by 20% to £20,000.

flexible budget report – assuming 80% output for one month

	budget	budget	actual	variance	trend
output level	100%	80%			
	£	£	£	£	
materials cost	100,000	80,000	81,000	(1,000)	ADV
labour cost	50,000	40,000	42,000	(2,000)	ADV
variable overheads	25,000	20,000	18,000	2,000	FAV
fixed overheads	25,000	25,000	26,000	(1,000)	ADV
TOTAL	200,000	165,000	167,000	(2,000)	ADV

setting new budgets

It is clear that budget monitoring is an on-going process. As we saw in the Case Study, budgets set for one financial year can be 'flexed' if the level of output of the business requires it.

When the time comes for budgets to be set for the *next* financial year there are two methods that can be used:

incremental budgets

In an *incremental budget* the previous year's budget figures are used as a basis and a small percentage added on (the 'increment') to allow for general rises in costs brought about by inflation. This type of budgeting works reasonably well in situations where the area budgeted for is stable – eg in local authorities – but has the major disadvantage that it does not analyse costs – inefficiences (overspending) remain in the system.

zero-based budgeting

The other alternative when setting budgets is to 'start from scratch'. The budget starts from zero, and each item going into the budget has to be justified by the budget holder – normally the manager of the department. This ensures that inefficiencies and overspending are avoided. It is, however, a time-consuming procedure, and is hardly feasible every year. Some businesses therefore adopt the policy of using zero-based budgeting from time-to-time and incremental ('adding a bit on') budgeting in the intervening years.

chapter summary

- Once budgets have been planned and put into action, they must be monitored so that the actual figures are compared with the budgeted figures.

- Responsibility for a budget is normally given to a departmental manager – the budget holder – as part of what is known as *responsibility accounting* for his or her budget centre.

- Variances – the difference between actual and budgeted figures – should only be acted upon if they are significant – a process known as management by exception. Control limits are set up for costs, so that significant variances can be identified.

- Budget reports are completed by budget holders for each budget period so that the management of the business can monitor performance.

- Flexible budgets are a series of fixed budgets for different levels of output of the business for a given budget period.

- Budgets for the new financial period can be set either on an incremental ('adding a bit on') basis or on a zero-based ('starting from scratch') system.

STUDENT ACTIVITIES

6.1 Briefly describe – using numbered steps – the processes of budget planning and budgetary control. Illustrate your description with a flow diagram.

6.2 What is *responsibility accounting*? What are its benefits? Find examples from local businesses of ways in which employees are rewarded for meeting (and/or improving upon) budget targets.

6.3 What is *management by exception* and how is it put into action? To which level of management (if any) should the following variances be reported and why? Choose from: director, departmental manager, supervisor.

(a) sales of Product A are 50% below budget in the first budget period of the year

(b) photocopying costs in the administration department are 15% above budget

(c) labour costs in the production department are 20% above budget

(d) National Insurance costs (employer's contribution) in the staffing budget have risen by 8%

In each case state the likely cause of the variance and suggest what action could be taken.

6.4 The annual budgets of Thorne Engineering Limited are made up of thirteen budget periods, each of four weeks in length. The administration department budget uses budget heads of staff, equipment, consumables, operating costs and expenses. The budget figures for the department for the first three budget periods of the financial year are as follows:

	PERIOD 1	PERIOD 2	PERIOD 3
	Budget	Budget	Budget
BUDGET HEAD	£	£	£
Staff	5,000	5,000	5,500
Equipment	–	10,000	2,000
Consumables	1,350	1,500	1,500
Operating costs and expenses	2,250	1,250	1,750

(a) You are to set out the administration department budget for each of the three budget periods (include columns for the actual and variance figures to be inserted later); year-to-date figures are not required. Use a computer spreadsheet if one is available.

(b)   The actual figures for the administration department expenditure are set out below. You are to complete the actual and variance columns for the budgets prepared in (a).

	PERIOD 1	PERIOD 2	PERIOD 3
	Actual	Actual	Actual
BUDGET HEAD	£	£	£
Staff	5,450	4,750	5,450
Equipment	2,000	9,000	3,500
Consumables	1,450	1,750	1,700
Operating costs and expenses	1,870	1,960	1,690

(c)   Prepare the year-to-date figures on separate pieces of paper, or computer printouts, for the three budget periods.

(d)   For each budget period prepare a report addressed to the administration department manager, who is the budget holder. The reports should highlight significant budget variances, suggesting the reasons for any variances and the corrective action to be taken.

(e)   Suggest an appropriate timescale for monitoring the budget based on the knowledge that the management of Thorne Engineering Limited hold a budget meeting on the Wednesday of week 3 of every budget period.

6.5   Lowman Products has set a fixed production budget for the first budget period of the financial year (Period 1). The actual figures were below budget however: materials cost £162,000, labour cost £84,000, variable overheads £36,000, fixed overheads £52,000.

You are to:

(a)   Set out a fixed budget report for Period 1 and calculate the variances (see page 92 for an example of a fixed budget report).

(b)   Set out a flexible budget report for Period 1 (see the format below), calculating the flexible budget figures at 80% of budgeted production. Enter the actual figures, calculate the variances and enter the trends.

(c)   Why are the trends shown by the variances in the fixed and flexible budgets different?

	budget	budget	actual	variance	trend
output level	100%	80%			
BUDGET HEAD	£	£	£	£	
materials cost	200,000				
labour cost	100,000				
variable overheads	50,000				
fixed overheads	50,000				
TOTAL	400,000				

EVIDENCE COLLECTION EXERCISE

Solban Limited – preparing and monitoring the sales budget

for BTEC Element 11.2
Explain and illustrate the key features of a budgetary planning system

INTRODUCTION

This Evidence Collection Exercise looks at the way Solban Limited, a manufacturer of sunglasses, plans to expands its sales by starting a mail order promotion in addition to its already successful supply to the retail trade. The tasks involve:

•   the preparation of sales budgets – for units of production and sales revenue
•   the preparation of a production budget to see if the planned sales can be met
•   monitoring of actual sales figures against the budget projections
•   analysis of variances to see how they will affect the operation of the business

Solban Limited
Solban Limited is a medium-sized company which manufactures a quality brand of sunglasses known as the 'SunSet'. It has traditionally supplied the major retail chains: the glasses normally sell for £20 and Solban receives £15 per pair after deduction of trade discount allowed to the stores.

the sales plan
Solban's management has been looking at ways of expanding sales, and has decided that selling direct by mail order will open up new markets. Advertising will be placed in the 'small ads' section of daily newspapers. The advantage of mail order is that the revenue received will be £20 per pair, rather than the £15 received from retail stockists.

The management has decided against any price rise. Sunglasses made by Solban's competitors range from a 'cheap and cheerful' type costing £10 to the up-market range costing £30 plus, or more. Solban's 'SunSet' at £20 provides quality and value for money. Forecasts show that more people in the UK are seeking the sun for their holidays: either in the winter (ski-ing and 'winter sun' holidays) or in the summer. Economic indicators show that people have more disposable income to spend on holidays. In short, prospects for the sale of sunglasses are encouraging.

sales projections

Solban's sales figures for last year (19-4) were by units (pairs of sunglasses):

January	5,000
February	4,000
March	3,000
April	3,500
May	6,500
June	12,000
July	14,500
August	9,500
September	1,500
October	2,500
November	4,500
December	4,500
TOTAL	71,000

Solban's management considers that it can sell:
- an extra 500 pairs of sunglasses each month by mail order – income £20 per pair
- the same number of pairs of glasses to retailers as in 19-4 – income £15 per pair

TASKS

1. Draw up a sales budget for 19-5 showing monthly sales of units (pairs of sunglasses) – use the format of the sales figures for 19-4 shown above, and show the total number of units to be produced.

2. Draw up a sales budget for 19-5 showing monthly sales income based on the prices which have been decided upon. List the months as in Task 1, and show the total expected sales income.

3. Draw up a production budget for 19-5 showing monthly production by unit, to see if the projected increase in sales can be met.
   The following factors have to be considered:
   - stock at 1 January is 8,500 units
   - maximum monthly output is 7,500 units
   - the maximum stock at the end of any one month should be 20,000 units

   Use the format shown on the next page. Remember that closing stock for one month is the opening stock for the following month.

Solban Limited – production budget for 19-5

UNITS	Jan	Feb	Mar	Apr	May	Jun	Jul	Aug	Sep	Oct	Nov	Dec
Opening stock												
add Units produced												
less Units sold												
Closing stock												

4. It is the first week of June of 19-5. The actual monthly sales figures for Solban sunglasses (in units) are as follows:

	retail sales	*mail order*
January	4,900	450
February	3,800	650
March	4,000	800
April	5,500	900
May	8,500	1,000

You are to draw up a budget report for May (see below) showing:
- the figures for the current period and variances
- year-to-date figures and the cumulative variances

Solban Limited – sales budget report for May 19-5

	May			*Year-to-date*		
	budget	actual	variance	budget	actual	variance
	£	£	£	£	£	£
Retail sales						
Mail order						
TOTAL SALES						

5. Draw up a report addressed to the sales manager, Mr A Patel, setting out:
    (a) a bar chart showing budgeted and actual sales for January to May
    (b) significant variances (ie in excess of a 10% control limit)

6. Write a memorandum from Mr Patel, the sales manager, to the managing director, Mr S. Schein, briefly setting out the implications of the variances for:
    (a) the production schedules
    (b) the cash flow of the business
    The memorandum should suggest a meeting of senior management as soon as possible.

Section

3

monitoring costs

7 Classification of costs

introduction

So far in this book we have looked at the budgeting process by which a business projects financial plans and targets. We now turn to a more detailed study of cost accounting, ie calculating how much it costs to make a product. Note that a 'product' can be a manufactured item or a service.

In this chapter we look at:
* *ways of classifying costs, ie different ways of showing the costs of a business in order to help with decision making*
* *the total cost statement, ie the calculation of the total cost of a product*

purpose of cost accounting

Cost accounting uses various techniques which enable a business to monitor the use of its financial resources. The information provided by cost accounting will help the managers of a business to assess performance and make decisions which will affect what the business does in the future, eg
* to manufacture more of one product than another
* to provide one service in preference to another
* to reduce costs
* to review selling prices
* to manufacture a new product, or provide a new service
* to close one department or division of the business

In later chapters we shall see how cost accounting is used in decision making; before this, though, we need to understand certain techniques of cost accounting. In this chapter, we begin our cost accounting by looking at the *classification of costs*.

classification of costs

Within any business, whether it manufactures a product or provides a service, there are certain costs involved at various stages to produce the *units of output*. By 'unit of output' we mean an item manufactured (eg a car), or a service provided (eg a client hour in a firm of accountants). The diagram which follows (fig 7.1) shows the costs of a manufacturing business which are incurred by the three main sections of the business, ie the factory, the warehouse, the office.

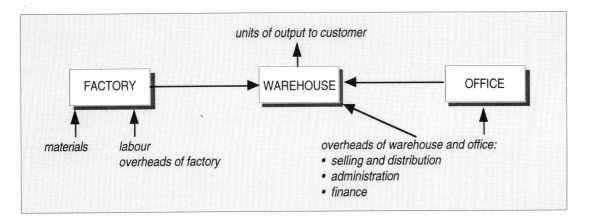

Fig. 7.1 Costs incurred in a manufacturing business

Note that while the above diagram shows the costs of a manufacturing business, it can be adapted easily to fit non-manufacturing organisations, such as a shop, a hospital, a school or college, a church, a youth club. While the units of output of these organisations differ from those of a manufacturer, nevertheless they still incur costs at various stages of the 'production' process.

Having identified costs for each main section of a business, we can now *classify the costs*. This can be done in three ways:

*   by element
*   by function
*   by nature

We will now explain each of these.

classification of costs by element

The diagram above shows that there are three elements of total cost:

*   materials, ie the cost of goods used
*   labour, ie the cost of employees' wages and salaries
*   expenses, ie other costs, mainly the overheads (see next page)

Each of the cost elements can be categorised between:

- *direct costs* – those costs that can be identified directly with each unit of output
- *indirect costs* – all other costs, ie those that cannot be identified with each unit of output

The cost elements for a manufacturing business now appear as:

MATERIALS	**direct**	materials from which the finished product is made
	indirect	other materials used in the factory, eg grease for machines, cleaning materials, etc

LABOUR	**direct**	wages paid to those who work the machinery on the production line or who are involved in assembly of the product
	indirect	wages and salaries paid to those who are not directly involved in production, eg supervisors, maintenance staff, etc

EXPENSES	**direct**	expenses which can be attributed to units of production, eg royalties payable to the designer of a product, special items bought in for a particular product
	indirect	other expenses, such as rent, business rates, telephone, lighting, heating, which cannot be attributed directly to production

Note that the *indirect* costs of materials, labour and expenses form the *overheads* of the business:

indirect materials + indirect labour + indirect expenses = total overheads

classification of costs by function

Each section of a business, eg factory, warehouse, office, performs a *function*. Thus, for example, the office provides an administrative function. In carrying out these functions, costs are incurred and can be classified by function. For a manufacturing business the main functions are:

- factory, or production
- selling and distribution
- administration
- finance

Other functions can be added to suit the needs of a particular business. For example, a company might spend large sums of money in researching and developing new products – the costs incurred by this function will be classified under the research and development heading.

Non-manufacturing organisations – such as a hospital or a college – will use some of the same functions listed above, and will add other, specialist, functions. Both direct and indirect costs can be classified by function. It is important to note that, when costs are classified by function, there are no extra costs to classifying by element: they are the same costs presented in a different way.

classification of costs by nature

It is important in cost accounting to appreciate the nature of costs – in particular to appreciate that not all costs increase or decrease directly in line with increases or decreases in output. By nature, costs are:

- fixed, or
- variable, or
- semi-variable

Fig. 7.2 shows the differences between these.

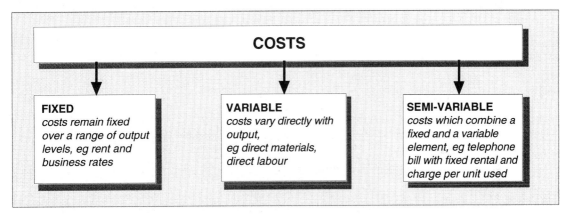

COSTS

FIXED
costs remain fixed over a range of output levels, eg rent and business rates

VARIABLE
costs vary directly with output, eg direct materials, direct labour

SEMI-VARIABLE
costs which combine a fixed and a variable element, eg telephone bill with fixed rental and charge per unit used

Fig. 7.2 Classifying costs by nature

We shall see in Chapter 11 "Break-even analysis" how a knowledge of the nature of costs can help in decision making.

reasons for classifying costs

You may ask, "Why classify costs in three ways?" The answer is that we can see the same business from three different viewpoints – this will help management to run the business better.

- ***by element***
  We are looking for the high cost elements in order to make savings, eg labour might be identified as being too high.

- ***by function***
  We look at the different departments to see which are the high-spending departments – perhaps savings can be made

- ***by nature***
  We identify the costs as being fixed, variable, or semi-variable. This will help with decision making – the business might be able to alter the balance between fixed and variable costs in order to increase profits.

total cost statement

The total cost statement lists all the costs involved in producing the output of a business. It can be prepared on the basis of:

- a single cost unit, eg the cost of making one car in a car factory
- a batch, eg the cost of making 1,000 'limited edition' cars
- the whole factory, eg the cost of all the car factory's output for a given time period

The total cost statement is prepared as follows:

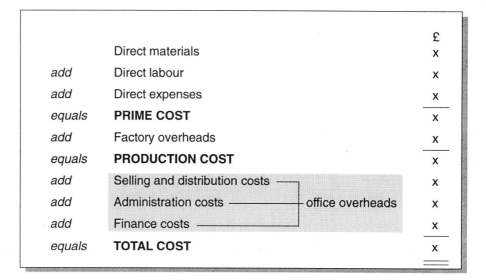

		£
	Direct materials	x
add	Direct labour	x
add	Direct expenses	x
equals	**PRIME COST**	x
add	Factory overheads	x
equals	**PRODUCTION COST**	x
add	Selling and distribution costs ┐	x
add	Administration costs ─────── office overheads	x
add	Finance costs ─────┘	x
equals	**TOTAL COST**	x

Note that:

- *prime cost* is the direct cost of manuracturing products, before the addition of factory overheads
- *production cost* is the factory cost of manufacturing the products, ie prime cost plus factory overheads
- *total cost* is production cost plus office overheads; note that total cost plus profit of the business equals the selling price of the products

As has been noted earlier in this chapter, the cost structure for other types of businesses will vary from that shown above for a manufacturing business.

By taking total cost away from sales revenue (ie money from goods sold) we can create a profit statement. This shows the profitability of the business after all costs have been taken into account. The profit statement is:

		£
	Sales	x
less	Total cost	x
equals	PROFIT	x

chapter summary

■ Cost accounting calculates how much it costs to produce a product.

■ All businesses incur costs to produce units of output.

■ Costs can be classified by element, by function and by nature

■ The main elements of cost are
  • materials
  • labour
  • expenses
  Each of these can be direct or indirect.

■ Costs can be classified by function, for example, factory, or production, selling and distribution, administration, finance

■ By nature, costs are fixed, or variable, or semi-variable.

■ A total cost statement lists all the direct costs and the overheads involved in producing the output of a business. Sales revenue minus total cost equals profit.

STUDENT ACTIVITIES

7.1 **(a)** What are the main areas of cost for the following organisations?
  – a shop
  – a hospital
  – a school or college
  – a church
  – a youth club

Prepare a diagram, similar to that shown on page 101, for each organisation listed above identifying the main functions of the organisation and the costs incurred by each section.

(b) Classify each of the following costs by nature (ie fixed, or variable, or semi-variable):
  • raw materials
  • factory rent
  • telephone
  • direct labour, eg production workers paid on a piecework basis
  • indirect labour, eg supervisors' salaries
  • commission paid to sales staff

Taking the costs in turn, explain to Louise Smith, who is about to set up a furniture manufacturing business, why you have classified each as fixed, or variable, or semi-variable. Answer her comment, "What difference does it make anyway, they are all costs that have to be paid."

7.2 Severn Manufacturing Co Ltd makes chairs for school and college use. The chairs have plastic seats, and tubular steel legs. The firm's cost accountant asks you to help her classify the manufacturing costs into:

- direct materials
- indirect materials
- direct labour
- indirect labour
- direct expenses
- indirect expenses

The costs to be classified are:

COST	CLASSIFICATION (write your answer)
Tubular steel	
Factory foreman's salary	
Wages of employee operating the moulding machine which produces the chair seats	
Works canteen assistant's wages	
Business rates of factory	
Power to operate machines	
Factory heating and lighting	
Plastic for making chair seats	
Hire of special machinery for one particular order	
Cost of oil for the moulding machine	
Rent of administrative office	
Depreciation of factory machinery	
Depreciation of office equipment	

7.3 Eveshore Pottery Co Ltd manufactures a range of 'souvenir' mugs, cups and saucers, plates, etc, which sell well to visitors from abroad who are seeking a reminder of 'Olde England'. A number of different costs have been incurred during the last month, and you are asked to assist the cost accountant by classifying them into:

- direct materials
- indirect materials
- direct labour

- indirect labour
- direct expenses
- indirect expenses

The costs are:
- cleaning materials for the machines
- wages of factory foreman
- clay from which the 'pots' are made
- 10p royalties payable to the designer for each 'Eveshore Plate' made
- salary of office clerk
- electricity used to heat the kilns
- business rates of factory
- depreciation of office equipment
- wages of production line workers
- salesman's salary
- interest charged on bank overdraft

Of the overhead costs, ie indirect materials, indirect labour, and indirect expenses, you are to indicate which would be classified as:

- factory overheads
- selling and distribution overheads
- administration overheads
- finance overheads

7.4 The following figures relate to the accounts of Hughes Ltd, a manufacturing business, for the year ended 31 December 19-1:

	£
Raw materials used in the factory	118,830
Rent and business rates	16,460
Factory wages	117,315
Factory power	3,825
Factory heat and light	1,185
Factory expenses and maintenance	4,095
Salaries and wages	69,350
Advertising	11,085
Office expenses	3,930
Depreciation of factory plant and machinery	3,725
Sales revenue	426,350

You are to prepare a total cost statement for the year which shows clearly:

(a) • prime cost
   • production cost
   • total cost

(b) a profit statement for the year

8

Costing systems

introduction

The previous chapter looked at how costs can be classified; in this chapter we see how costs are collected together and presented in order to provide information to the managers of a business. In particular, we shall look at the costing systems of:

- *absorption costing*
- *marginal costing*
- *standard costing*
- *activity based costing*

As we will see, each of these is used to assist managers in running the business more efficiently, and to aid their decision making.

cost units and cost centres

Before we begin our study of costing systems we need to understand the costing terms: *cost units* and *cost centres*.

Cost units are units of output to which costs can be charged.

A cost unit can be

- *either* a unit of production from a factory such as a car, a television, an item of furniture
- *or* a unit of service, such as a passenger-mile on a bus, a transaction on a bank statement, an attendance at a swimming pool

Cost centres are sections of a business to which costs can be charged

A cost centre in a manufacturing business, for example, is a department of a factory, a particular stage in the production process, or even a whole factory. In a college, examples of cost centres are the teaching departments, or particular sections of departments, the school or college administrative office. In a hospital, examples of cost centres are the hospital wards, operating theatres, specialist sections such as the X-ray department, pathology department.

what costing systems are used?

In this chapter we will look at the costing systems of:

- absorption costing
- marginal costing
- standard costing
- activity based costing

Fig 8.1, below, shows the purpose of each of these costing systems. The use of each costing system is dependent on the information needs of the business:

-     is a profit figure needed? (use absorption costing)
-     can we afford to sell 1,000 units each month to Megastores Limited at a discount of 20 per cent? (use marginal costing)
-     why are the overheads so high for the production line making 'Product X'? (use activity based costing)
-     how much will it cost us to make 'Product Y' next month? (use standard costing)

Note that absorption costing, marginal costing, and activity based costing are all systems that can be used in conjunction with standard costing, if required.

In the remainder of this chapter we will consider each costing system in more detail.

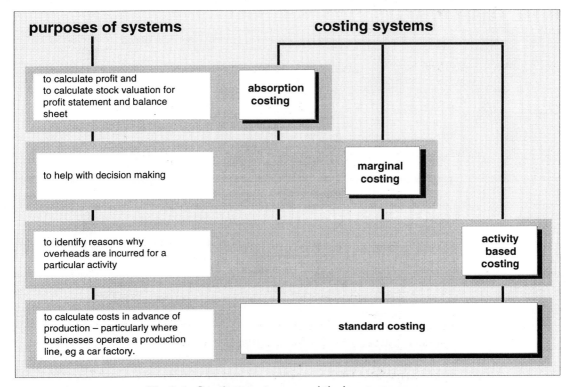

Fig 8.1 Costing systems and their purposes

absorption costing

Absorption costing absorbs the total costs of the whole business into each cost unit. It answers the question, "What does it cost to make one unit of output?"

The absorption cost of a unit of output is made up of the following costs:

		£
	direct materials	x
add	direct labour	x
add	direct expenses	x
add	overheads (fixed and variable)	x
equals	ABSORPTION COST	x

Notes:

- As you will remember from the previous chapter, the overheads of a business comprise both the factory and the office costs of indirect materials, indirect labour, and indirect expenses.

- Under some circumstances, absorption costing includes only production costs, ie it excludes all costs beyond production, such as selling and distribution costs, administration costs, and finance costs.

example

The Wyvern Bike Company makes 100 bikes each week, and its costs are as follows:

weekly costs for producing 100 bikes

	£
direct materials (£20 per bike)	2,000
direct labour (£25 per bike)	2,500
PRIME COST	4,500
overheads (fixed)	3,500
TOTAL COST	8,000

Notes:

- there are no direct expenses incurred by the company
- the selling price of each bike is £100, which gives a profit statement of:

		£
	selling price (100 bikes x £100)	10,000
less	total cost	8,000
equals	PROFIT	2,000

The absorption cost of producing one bike is:

$$\frac{\text{total cost}}{\text{number of cost units}} = \frac{£8,000}{100 \text{ bikes}} = £80 \text{ per bike}$$

As you will see from the above example, each cost unit bears an equal proportion of the costs of the overheads of the business. Because of its simplicity, absorption costing is a widely used system which tells us how much it costs to make one unit of output. It works well where the cost units are all identical, eg 100 identical bikes, but is less appropriate where some of the cost units differ in quality, eg 100 bikes, of which 75 are standard models and 25 are handbuilt to the customers' specifications. It also ignores the effect of changes in the level of output on the cost structure. For example, if the bike manufacturer reduces output to 50 bikes a week:

- will direct materials remain at £20 per bike? (buying materials in smaller quantities might mean higher prices)
- will direct labour still be £25 per bike? (with less production, the workforce may not be able to specialise in certain jobs, and may be less efficient)
- will the overheads remain fixed at £3,500? (perhaps smaller premises can be used and the factory rent reduced)

marginal costing

Marginal costing is the cost of producing one extra unit of output

As we have seen in the previous chapter costs, by nature, are:
- *fixed*, ie they do not vary with changes in the number of units of output produced
  or
- *variable*, ie they vary in line with the number of units produced
  or
- *semi-variable*, ie they combine both a fixed and a variable element

For most purposes, marginal costing is not concerned with fixed costs (such as the rent of a factory); it is concerned with variable costs – direct materials, direct labour, direct expenses, and variable factory overheads – which increase when production increases. For most decision making, the marginal cost of a unit of production is, therefore, the prime cost of making one more unit.

example
Continuing with the example of the Wyvern Bike Company, the marginal cost per unit is:

	£	
direct materials	20	per bike
direct labour	25	per bike
MARGINAL COST	45	per bike

It therefore costs £45 to produce one extra bike.

Knowing the marginal cost of a unit enables the management of a business to focus their attention on the *contribution* provided by each unit. The contribution is the amount of money coming in to the business from sales after marginal costs have been paid.

The contribution in the case of the Wyvern Bike Company is:

		£
	selling price of one bike	100
less	marginal cost of producing one bike	45
equals	CONTRIBUTION per bike	55

The contribution, as its name implies, contributes to the costs of the overheads (running expenses) of the business. Once these are covered, the remainder of contribution is profit. Thus the calculation for the Wyvern Bike Company's weekly production of 100 bikes is:

		£
	selling price	10,000
less	marginal cost	4,500
equals	CONTRIBUTION	5,500
less	overheads (fixed)	3,500
equals	PROFIT	2,000

You will note that absorption costing and marginal costing give two different costs per bike for the Wyvern Bike Company: under absorption costing it is £80 per bike, while marginal costing gives £45. At a level of production of 100 bikes per week, both costing systems show a profit of £2,000. You might say, "What is the difference between the two systems?" Supposing that the owner of the Wyvern Bike Company, as a friend, says to you, "I'll make one extra bike next week for you, and you can have it at cost price." Which price do you think you should pay: £80 or £45? The answer is, of course, at the marginal cost. (If you want to pay £80, try reworking the cost statement, on the previous page, based on 101 bikes, and then calculate the profit.) Knowing the marginal cost of production helps with management decision making. In Chapter 10, we shall come back to marginal costs and see how they are used in making pricing decisions for 'special orders'.

Where a company has a number of different products, the marginal costing system can be used to calculate the contribution of each. In this way management can seek to maximise the contribution (and ultimately the profit) by selling more of the higher contribution products.

example

The Avon Manufacturing Company makes three products: X, Y and Z. Details are as follows:

		X	Y	Z
		£	£	£
	selling price (per unit)	60	50	40
less	marginal cost (per unit)	30	30	30
equals	CONTRIBUTION (per unit)	30	20	10

If there is unlimited demand for each product and the company is able to switch production freely between the products without an increase in overheads, then the company should concentrate on product X only. (Product X has the highest contribution to sales percentage [£30 ÷ £60 x 100] of 50 per cent; product Y has 40 per cent; while product Z has 25 per cent.)

However, life is never that simple! It is almost certain that the number of units that the company can sell is limited, that the capacity of the factory is limited, and that, by making a mix of products, production is more efficient (eg materials common to all; perhaps product Z uses waste products from X and Y). Also, if production of one product is stopped, current buyers of the full range of products may take all their business to a rival manufacturer.

In a similar way to a manufacturing company, a department store can use marginal costing to calculate the contribution of each department. However, as with the manufacturing example above, care must be taken in interpreting the results – for example, closure of a department selling furniture would most probably adversely affect the sales of a carpet department.

linkage to stock valuation methods

In this section, and before we move on to the other costing methods, we will examine the linkage of absorption costing and marginal costing to the stock valuation methods of a business.

You will recall from your study of profit statements that 'closing stock' is the value of stock which remains unsold at the end of the financial year.

Using the two costing systems that we have studied so far in this chapter, closing stock is valued in the following way:

- *absorption costing*, at production cost (ie direct materials, direct labour, direct expenses, and factory overheads)
- *marginal costing*, at marginal production cost, ie
  - direct materials
  - direct labour
  - direct expenses
  - variable factory overheads

Note that both methods exclude office overheads and that, under marginal costing, fixed factory overheads are excluded.

The Case Study, which follows, shows the linkage of absorption costing and marginal costing to stock valuation methods, and the effect on profit.

CASE STUDY: CHAIRS LIMITED

situation

Chairs Limited commenced business on 1 January 19-1; it manufactures a special type of chair designed to alleviate back pain. The cost statement for the first year's trading, when 500 chairs were made, is as follows:

	£
Direct materials (£15 per chair)	7,500
Direct labour (£20 per chair)	10,000
PRIME COST	17,500
Factory overheads (fixed)	5,000
PRODUCTION COST	22,500
Office overheads (fixed)	5,000
TOTAL COST	27,500

Notes:

- there are no direct expenses incurred by the company
- the selling price of each chair is £100, and 400 were sold in the year with sales revenue of £40,000 (ie 400 chairs at £100)
- closing stock is 100 chairs (ie 500 made, less 400 sold)

What will be the valuation of the closing stock under absorption costing and marginal costing? Show the profit statements for the year under each costing system?

solution

Absorption costing

Closing stock is valued at production cost. To make 500 chairs, the production cost was £22,500 (see cost statement). This gives a production cost of £45 per chair (£22,500 ÷ 500 chairs). Closing stock, therefore, will be:

100 chairs at production cost of £45 = £4,500

Marginal costing

Closing stock is valued at marginal production cost. In this example, as the factory overheads are stated to be a fixed cost, the marginal cost comprises direct materials (£15 per chair) and direct labour (£20 per chair), giving a valuation of £35 per chair. Closing stock, therefore, will be:

100 chairs at marginal cost of £35 = £3,500

Profit statement: absorption costing

	£	£
sales		40,000
direct materials	7,500	
direct labour	10,000	
PRIME COST	17,500	
factory overheads	5,000	
	22,500	
less closing stock (see above)	4,500	
PRODUCTION COST	18,000	
office overheads	5,000	
TOTAL COST		23,000
PROFIT		17,000

Profit statement: marginal costing

	£	£
sales		40,000
direct materials	7,500	
direct labour	10,000	
	17,500	
less closing stock (see above)	3,500	
PRIME COST	14,000	
factory overheads	5,000	
PRODUCTION COST	19,000	
office overheads	5,000	
TOTAL COST		24,000
PROFIT		16,000

Notes:

- The difference in profit is solely because of the different closing stock valuations under the two costing systems.
- Under absorption costing, because one-fifth of the year's production remains in stock, one-fifth of the fixed factory overheads (£5,000 ÷ 5 = £1,000) is transferred into next year's profit statement. This is the reason why absorption costing shows a £1,000 higher profit for the year.
- By contrast, under marginal costing, the full amount of the factory overheads has been shown in this year's profit statement.
- If, at the end of its second year of trading, Chairs Limited has no closing stock, the profit difference will reverse, with marginal costing showing a £1,000 higher profit. This is because, under marginal costing, there is not the £1,000 of factory overheads brought forward from the first year.
- Under both methods, office overheads are shown in full in the profit statement.

For the purposes of financial accounts (ie for submission to the Inland Revenue for tax purposes and, in a limited company, to the shareholders) the absorption cost method is the usual basis for valuing stock. For internal use accounts (ie for the use of the management of the business), either the absorption cost or marginal cost methods can be used. The marginal cost method is especially important because it can be used for management decision making. We have already seen this earlier in the chapter, and we will look further at this aspect in Chapters 10, 11 and 12.

standard costing

Standard costing sets a pre-determined cost for materials, labour and overheads for the period ahead.

All businesses need methods of controlling the costs of materials, labour and overheads that go to make up the finished product (we have seen, in earlier chapters, how budgets can be set and controlled). Imagine a car factory where the cost and amount of materials to make the car is not known; where the hours of work and rates of pay are not known, where the cost of overheads is not known. Under such circumstances, the costs could not be controlled, and it would be impossible to quote a price for the product to a customer. Therefore many businesses establish a standard cost for their output. Thus a standard cost can be calculated for such things as diverse as a product manufactured in a factory, a hospital operation, servicing a car, a meal in a restaurant.

The standard cost for units of output is calculated in advance of producing the output and working on the assumption of either an ideal standard (ie no poor quality material, no overtime worked, no machine breakdowns), or a normal standard, which allows for a pre-determined amount of loss or wastage and a given level of efficiency.

Standard costs are set for:

* *materials*
  The quantity of each material to be used in production, and the price of such materials is pre-determined. Standard materials cost is the expected quantity of materials multiplied by expected material price.

* *labour*
  The labour hours required to manufacture a quantity of goods, and the cost of the labour is pre-determined. Standard labour cost is the expected labour hours multiplied by expected wage rates.

* *overheads*
  The expected quantity of output within a time period divided into the expected overheads will determine the standard overhead cost.

Once a standard cost has been established, it can be used as a method of cost control through variance analysis (see Chapter 9), and also for making pricing decisions (see Chapter 10). Note that standard costing is used in conjunction with absorption costing or marginal costing, ie the standard cost is set in advance of production using either absorption costing or marginal costing systems.

setting standards

In standard costing, it is important that care should be taken over the setting of standards. Poorly set standards will be worse than useless to the management of a business when the figures are used in further analysis.

The main departments within an organisation which can provide information to enable standards to be set are:

- *Purchasing*
  The buying department of a business will be able to determine prices, and their future trends, of materials used.

- *Personnel*
  This department will have current wage and salary rates, together with bonus and overtime details, of the various grades of employees; forecasts of changes can also be ascertained.

- *Management services*
  Often called work study, this department will determine the standard amount of time that each work-task in the production process should take.

- *Production*
  This department has overall responsibility for production and will know the quantities of raw materials required for each unit of production, and the value of production will be linked to the overhead costs.

CASE STUDY: DMS ENGINEERING LIMITED

situation

This company manufactures car bumper mouldings. It has been asked by its major customer, Okassa (Japan) Ltd to prepare a quotation for mouldings for a new car, which is code-named "OK10". The elements of cost for 100 mouldings have been calculated by DMS Engineering as:

materials	polycarbonate (of specified quality), 200 kilos at £1.10 perkilo matt black finishing material, 10 litres at £5.40 per litre
labour:	10 hours at £5.75 per hour 3 hours at £8.50 per hour
overheads:	factory and office, 13 hours at £20 per hour

Calculate:

- the standard cost of producing 100 bumper mouldings

- if DMS Engineering Ltd add 20% on to the standard cost, what will be the selling price of one bumper moulding it will quote to its customer?

solution

	£	£
materials		
polycarbonate: 200 kilos at £1.10 per kilo	220.00	
finishing material: 10 litres at £5.40 per litre	54.00	
		274.00
labour		
10 hours at £5.75	57.50	
3 hours at £8.50	25.50	
		83.00
		357.00
overheads (factory and office)		
13 hours at £20 per hour		260.00
STANDARD COST		617.00
profit (20% of standard cost)		123.40
TOTAL SELLING PRICE		740.40

Therefore one bumper sells for £740.40 ÷ 100 = £7.40.

activity based costing

Activity based costing charges overheads to output on the basis of activities.

Activity based costing is a relatively new costing system which adopts a different approach to charging overheads to output. It shows the reason why overheads are incurred by output, rather than the amount of overheads for a particular period.

Traditionally, costing systems have charged overheads to output on the basis of direct labour hours (or labour cost), or machine hours. For example, for each labour hour – or machine hour – required by the output £x of overheads is charged through an *overhead absorption rate*. While this method may be suitable for industries which are labour intensive, or where production requires the use of heavy machinery, it is not always appropriate for today's capital intensive, low-labour industries, as the example which follows will show.

example

A company manufactures two products, X and Y. Product X is produced on a labour-intensive production line, using basic machinery; product Y is produced using the latest 'state of the art' computer-controlled machinery, which requires few employees.

The company's elements of cost are:

direct materials, total	£500,000
– product X	£250,000
– product Y	£250,000
direct labour, total	£250,000
– product X	£200,000
– product Y	£50,000
overheads (fixed), total	£250,000

– a major proportion of these relate to maintenance and depreciation of the computer controlled machinery used to make product Y

The company uses labour cost as the basis by which to charge overheads to production. Therefore, the overhead will be split between the two products as:

overhead for product X = four-fifths of total overheads of £250,000 = £200,000
overhead for product Y = one-fifth of total overheads of £250,000 = £50,000

Thus, the majority of the overhead is charged to the labour-intensive production line (product X), and relatively little to the capital intensive line (product Y). As a major proportion of the costs relates to product Y, this has the effect of undercosting this product (and overcosting product X). Instead, a more appropriate costing method is needed.

the use of cost drivers

Cost drivers are activities which cause costs to be incurred

In the example looked at above, the cost driver used to charge overheads to output was – inappropriately – labour costs. Instead of using a cost driver linked to the volume of business (as above), activity based costing uses cost drivers linked to the *way in which business is conducted:* this concept is illustrated in the example which follows:

example

A company manufactures two products, A and B. Product A is produced in batches of 500 units of output; product B is produced in batches of 100 units of output. Each unit of production – whether A or B – requires one direct labour hour.

Production of each batch of A and B requires the following overheads:
- the machinery to be set-up at a cost of £400 per batch (to cover the engineer's time, test running of the machinery, etc)
- quality inspection at a cost of £200 per batch (to cover the inspector's time, cost of rejects, etc)

In a typical week the company produces 500 units of product A, ie one batch of 500 units, and 500 units of product B, ie five batches of 100 units. Thus the set-up and quality inspection costs for the week will be:

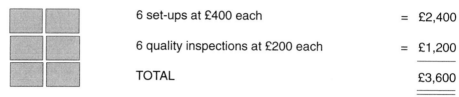

6 set-ups at £400 each	= £2,400
6 quality inspections at £200 each	= £1,200
TOTAL	£3,600

Note: each 'box' represents one set-up *and* one quality inspection

As each unit of output requires one direct labour hour, ie product A 500 hours, product B 500 hours, the overhead costs of set-ups and quality inspection, using traditional costing systems, will be charged to output as follows:

product A	= £1,800
product B	= £1,800
TOTAL	£3,600

We can see that this is an incorrect basis on which to charge overheads to output, because product A required just one set-up and one quality inspection, while product B took five set-ups and five quality inspections. By using the system of activity based costing, with set-up and inspection as cost drivers, we can charge overheads as follows:

product A

1 set-up at £400	= £400
1 quality inspection at £200	= £200
TOTAL	£600

product B

5 set-ups at £400	= £2,000
5 quality inspections at £200	= £1,000
TOTAL	£3,000

By using the activity based costing system, there is a more accurate reflection of the cost of demand on the support functions of set-up and quality inspection: it reduces the cost of 500 units of product A by £1,200 (ie £1,800 – £600) and increases the cost of 500 units of product B by £1,200 (ie from £1,800 to £3,000). This may have implications for the viability of product B, and for the selling price of both products.

other cost drivers

Cost drivers must have a close relationship with an activity, which can then be related to output. In the example we have seen the cost of set-ups and quality inspections as cost drivers. Examples of other activities and their cost drivers include:

activity	cost driver
• processing orders to suppliers	• number of orders
• processing invoices received from suppliers	• number of invoices
• processing orders to customers	• number of orders
• processing invoices issued to customers	• number of invoices

As has been seen in the example above, by using activity based costing, the emphasis is placed on which activities cause costs. It answers the question why costs are incurred, instead of simply stating the amount of the cost for a given period.

chapter summary

■ Absorption costing absorbs the total costs of the whole business into each cost unit.

■ Marginal costing is the cost of producing one extra unit of output.

■ Selling price less marginal cost equals contribution.

■ For the purposes of financial accounts, absorption cost is the basis used for stock valuation; for the purposes of management decision making, marginal cost shows the marginal cost of the stock.

■ Standard costing sets a pre-determined cost for materials, labour and overheads for the period ahead.

■ Activity based costing charges overheads to output on the basis of activities; it uses cost drivers (activities which cause costs to be incurred) to charge overheads to output.

STUDENT ACTIVITIES

8.1   John Walker Limited manufactures high quality training shoes (trainers). The management of the company is considering next year's production and has asked you, as cost clerk, to help with certain financial decisions.

The following information is available:

wholesale selling price (per pair)	£40
direct materials (per pair)	£15
direct labour (per pair)	£12
overheads (fixed)	£245,000 per year

The company is planning to manufacture 25,000 pairs of trainers next year.

You are to:

(a) calculate the absorption cost per pair of trainers

(b) calculate the marginal cost per pair of trainers

(c) prepare a profit statement to show the profit or loss if 25,000 pairs of trainers are sold

8.2   SuperSound Limited commenced business on 1 January 19-3, making small personal stereos. In 19-3 the company's production and sales were:

number of stereos manufactured	11,000
number of stereos sold	9,000

Sales were made at a constant price of £10 per stereo. The company's costs in 19-3 were:

	£
Direct materials	14,300
Direct labour	18,700
Factory overheads (fixed)	48,000
Office overheads (fixed)	20,000

You are to:

(a)   value the closing stock of SuperSound Limited at 31 December 19-3 using:
  • absorption costing
  • marginal costing

(b)   comment on the reason for the different valuations calculated in (a)

(c)   prepare profit statements for 19-3 using:
  • absorption costing
  • marginal costing

8.3   Rowcester Engineering Limited makes engine castings for a major car manufacturer. The castings are made in the foundry and are then sent to the machine shop for machining to the customer's specifications.

As a cost clerk, you have been asked to prepare a standard cost based on production of 100 castings. The following information is available to you:

- materials for 100 castings
    - 550 kg of ordinary steel at £3.50 per kg
    - 200 kg of high tensile steel at £10.00 per kg

- labour for 100 castings
    - 60 hours of foundry-workers' wages at £10.50 per hour
    - 155 hours in the machine shop at £12.75 per hour

- overheads (factory and office)
    - 210 hours at £25 per hour

You are to:

(a)   calculate the standard cost of producing 100 castings

(b)   if Rowcester Engineering adds 20% profit on to the standard cost, what will be the selling price of one casting?

8.4   Mereford Manufacturing Limited makes two products, A and B. Product A is made in batches of 10,000 units, and Product B is made in batches of 1,000 units. Each batch has the following set-up and quality inspection costs:
- set-up   £250
- quality inspection   £150

Each week, the company produces 50,000 units of A and 50,000 units of B. At present the company charges overheads to output on the basis of labour hours which are 500 hours per week for A and 500 hours for B.

You are to:

(a)   calculate the overheads charged to A and B each week, on the basis of labour hours

(b)   calculate the overheads charged to A and B each week, using activity based costing with the cost drivers of set-up and quality inspection

(c)   advise the management of Mereford Manufacturing Limited which is the more appropriate method of charging overheads to output

9 Monitoring costs through variance analysis

introduction

We have studied budgeting and costing in some detail already. We have seen in Chapter 6 the way in which budgets are monitored, Chapter 7 looked at the costs of making a product, and Chapter 8 was concerned with costing systems.

In this chapter we shall see how a business uses a standard costing system (see Chapter 8) as a method of monitoring costs through variance analysis. We shall look at:

- *the use of variance analysis*
- *monitoring costs*
- *variances and sub-variances, including the reasons for variances*
- *the use of a standard cost report in order to monitor variances*
- *the calculation of materials variances*
- *the calculation of labour variances*
- *overheads variances*

the use of variance analysis

We saw in the previous chapter how the standard costing system (pages 116-117) is used to set pre-determined costs for materials, labour and overheads. In this way, a business is able to calculate the cost of output in advance of production – an important factor in the budgetary process. Standard costing is almost invariably used as a method of cost control by comparing the actual cost of the output after it has been produced to establish the variance, ie

| standard cost | *minus* | actual cost | *equals* | variance |

monitoring costs

A business using the standard costing system will monitor the outcomes by comparing the standard costs set with the results that actually occurred. An outline of the monitoring process is shown in fig 9.1 below:

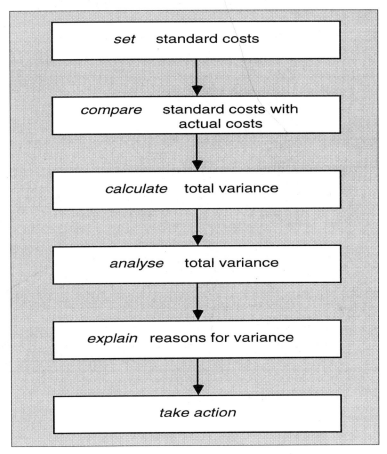

Fig 9.1 The monitoring process for standard costs

As we have seen already in chapter 6 (page 86), variances can be either favourable or adverse:

- a favourable (FAV) variance is when actual costs are lower than standard costs
- an adverse (ADV) variance is when actual costs are higher than standard costs

variances and sub-variances

The full amount by which the actual cost of a product differs from the standard cost is known as the total cost variance. It is calculated by deducting actual cost from standard cost, for example:

costs of making 300 garden gnomes

	£
standard cost	1,300
actual cost	1,405
TOTAL COST VARIANCE	105 ADV

The total cost variance is made up of the variances for each of the main elements of cost:

- materials
- labour
- overheads

The variance for each element can be further analysed into a number of sub-variances which are used to identify the *reasons* for the variance. Once the reasons have been identified, the management of the business can take action to ensure that they do not happen again.

The main variances and sub-variances for a manufacturing business are shown in fig 9.2 which follows.

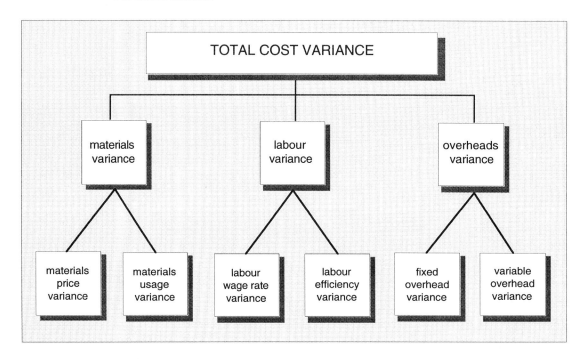

Fig 9.2 Variances and sub-variances for a manufacturing business

As the diagram shows, the total cost variance can result from a combination of different factors:

- *materials variance*
  - a price rise (or price fall) in the cost of materials
  - a change in the amount of materials used
- *labour variance*
  - an unexpected rise in pay rates, or the need to use a different grade of employee (at a higher or lower wage rate)
  - a change in efficiency levels, ie a higher or lower output than expected
- *overheads variance*
  - an unexpected change in fixed costs, such as an increase in the rent of the factory
  - a change in the cost or use of a variable overhead, such as electricity

Later in the chapter we will see how these variance factors – or sub-variances – can be identified and calculated. The principle of variance analysis is that variances and sub-variances are identified and calculated until they can be seen to be the responsibility of an individual employee, or small section within the business. For example, a materials price variance, where the cost of materials is different from the standard cost, is the responsibility of the buying department; it is this department that will have to explain to management the reason(s) for any variance.

standard cost report and monitoring variances

The variances for each cost element are summarised on a standard cost report, which takes a similar format to the budgetary control report already seen in chapter 6 (fig 6.4 on page 88). An example of a standard cost report is shown below (fig 9.3).

STANDARD COST REPORT

product   300 garden gnomes   **date**   07.11.19-5

supervisor   Richard Clay   **period**   October 19-5

	current period			trend	comments
	standard cost £	actual cost £	variance £		
materials	300	270	30	FAV	
labour	600	750	150	ADV	
overheads:					
fixed	300	275	25	FAV	
variable	100	110	10	ADV	
TOTAL COST	1,300	1,405	105	ADV	

Fig 9.3 Format of a standard cost report

The standard cost report shows the variances for each cost element. A favourable variance is a positive amount, eg for materials £300 – £270 = £30 FAV. Because actual costs are lower than standard, a favourable variance increases profits. By contrast, an adverse variance, eg labour £600 – £750 = £150 ADV, adds to costs and so reduces profits.

It is for the management of the business to decide which variances need further investigation – in the report shown in fig 9.3 it seems most likely that the labour cost will be looked at.

sub-variances

As mentioned in the previous section of this chapter, within the cost elements there is likely to be a combination of different factors causing each variance. Principally these factors – or *sub-variances* – are concerned with:

- price or rate, ie the price of materials, or the rate at which employees are paid
- usage or efficiency, ie the amount of materials used, or the efficiency of the employees

In order to calculate the sub-variances for materials and labour we need to know the make-up of both the standard and the actual cost in terms of

- materials: price and usage
- labour: rate and efficiency

Sub-variances can also be calculated for overheads, although we shall not be covering these in this book. It is the procedures for monitoring costs and the factors that can cause sub-variances that are important. Fig 9.4 shows how the standard cost report for 300 garden gnomes (seen earlier in fig 9.3) can be developed to show the sub-variances.

	standard cost		actual cost		sub-variances		
		£		£		£	£
materials	600 kilos		450 kilos		price	45	ADV
	at 50p per kilo	300	at 60p per kilo	270	usage	75	FAV
						30	FAV
labour	100 hours		150 hours		rate	150	FAV
	at £6.00 per hour	600	at £5.00 per hour	750	efficiency	300	ADV
						150	ADV
overheads							
fixed		300		275		*25	FAV
variable		100		110		*10	ADV
TOTAL COST		1,300		1,405		105	ADV

* sub-variances not calculated here (see text)

Fig 9.4 Standard cost report, showing sub-variances for materials and labour

From the report, the labour sub-variances will certainly cause the management to investigate the reasons for both the favourable and adverse variances.

In the next two sections we will see how the sub-variances are calculated for materials and labour. The figures which will be used in the Case Studies relate to the standard cost reports shown in figs 9.3 and 9.4. However, in order to give a clear explanation, the sub-variances are calculated on a 'per unit' basis. To check sub-variances back to the standard cost reports, simply multiply by 300 (because the standard cost reports are for 300 units of output).

the calculation of materials variances

As we have seen in fig 9.2, the variances and sub-variances for materials costs are:

variance
- materials variance, *which is caused by*

sub-variances
- materials *price* variance – the price paid
- materials *usage* variance – the amount used

The money amounts of these are calculated from the areas indicated in the diagram set out below. Note that, for clarity of presentation, both the actual price and the actual quantity used are *greater* than standard, ie they are adverse variances.

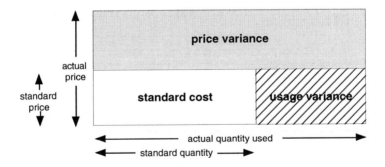

The variances are calculated as follows:

materials variance =
(standard quantity x standard price) – (actual quantity x actual price)

This variance can then be analysed further by calculating the *sub-variances:*

materials price sub-variance =
(standard price – actual price) x actual quantity

materials usage sub-variance =
(standard quantity – actual quantity) x standard price

notes from the diagram

- The change in the price of materials, based on the quantity actually used, forms the materials price variance – shaded [   ] in the diagram. This variance is the responsibility of the buying department.

- The change in the actual quantity used, based on the standard price, forms the materials usage variance – shaded ⬚ in the diagram. This variance is the responsibility of the production department.

- As noted, for clarity of presentation, the diagram shows adverse price and usage variances; these variances can also be favourable, ie less than the standard cost.

CASE STUDY: CALCULATING MATERIALS VARIANCES

situation

A manufacturer of clay garden gnomes has prepared the following information:
- the standard price of clay used to make the gnomes is 50p per kilo
- the standard usage is 2 kilos per gnome

The results achieved for last month's production are:
- the actual price of clay used was 60p per kilo
- the actual usage was 1.5 kilos per gnome

In short, the clay has cost more, but less has been used for each gnome.

What are the variances and sub-variances for materials costs?

solution

Here both the price and usage have differed from the standard to give the following *materials variance:*

(standard quantity x   standard price) – (actual quantity x actual price)

(2 kgs x 50p per kg)	–	(1.5 kgs x 60p per kg) =
£1.00	–	90p	= £0.10 FAVOURABLE

While the materials variance is favourable by £0.10, as both price *and* usage differ from standard, the sub-variances must be calculated:

Materials price sub-variance
(standard price – actual price)   x   actual quantity

(50p x 60p)	x	1.5 kgs	= £0.15 ADVERSE

Materials usage sub-variance
(standard quantity – actual quantity) x   standard price

(2 kgs – 1.5 kgs)	x	50p	= £0.25 FAVOURABLE

MATERIALS VARIANCE	£0.10 FAVOURABLE

For a production run of 300 garden gnomes, the materials variance is £30 FAV (300 x 10p). This agrees with the standard cost report shown in fig 9.3. As a consequence, the rise in price (the adverse sub-variance) must be investigated.

the calculation of labour variances

The variances and sub-variances for labour costs (see fig 9.2) are:

variance
- labour variance, *which is caused by*

sub-variances
- labour rate variance – the rate of wages paid
- labour efficiency variance – the level of efficiency of the workforce

The money amounts of these are calculated from the areas indicated in the diagram set out below. Note that for clarity of presentation, both actual wage rate and the actual hours worked are greater than standard, ie they are adverse variances:

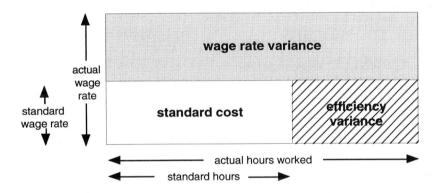

The variances are calculated as follows:

labour variance =
(standard hours x standard rate) – (actual hours x actual rate)

This variance can then be analysed further by calculating the *sub-variances:*

labour wage rate sub-variance =
(standard rate – actual rate) x actual hours

labour efficiency sub-variance =
(standard hours – actual hours) x standard rate

notes from the diagram:
- The change in the labour wage rate, based on the actual hours worked, forms the labour rate variance – shaded [   ] in the diagram. This variance is the responsibility of the personnel department.

- The change in the actual hours worked, based on the standard hours, forms the labour efficiency variance – shaded ///// in the diagram. This variance is the responsibility of the production department.

CASE STUDY: CALCULATING LABOUR VARIANCES

situation

A manufacturer of clay garden gnomes has prepared the following information:

- the standard cost of direct labour is £6.00 per hour
- the standard efficiency is production of one gnome every 20 minutes (0.333 of an hour)

The results achieved for last month's production are:

- the actual cost of direct labour was £5.00 per hour
- the actual production was one gnome every 30 minutes (0.5 of an hour)

In short, the wage rates are lower, but the employees have not worked as efficiently.

What are the variances and sub-variances for labour costs?

solution

Here both the rate and efficiency have differed from the standard to give the following *labour variance:*

(standard hours x standard rate) – (actual hours x actual rate)

(0.333 hours x £6.00 per hour) – (0.5 hours x £5.00 per hour) =
    £2.00   –   £2.50   = £0.50 ADVERSE

Note: The calculation gives a negative figure of 50p; this means that the actual cost is more than the standard cost, ie it is adverse, and profits will reduce. By contrast, a favourable cost variance is a positive figure, ie the actual cost is less than the standard cost, and profits will increase.

While the overall labour variance is adverse by 50p, as both rate and efficiency differ from standard, the sub-variances must be calculated:

Labour rate sub-variance

(standard rate – actual rate)   *x   actual hours*
(£6.00 – £5.00)   x 0.5 hours   = £0.50 FAVOURABLE

Labour efficiency sub-variance

(standard hours – actual hours)   x   standard rate
(0.333 hours – 0.5 hours)   x £6.00   = £1.00 ADVERSE

LABOUR VARIANCE   = £0.50 ADVERSE

For a production run of 300 garden gnomes, the labour variance is £150 ADV (300 x 50p). This agrees with the standard cost report shown in fig 9.3.

overhead variances

Overhead variances take into account the fixed and variable nature of costs. The variances for overheads (see fig 9.2) are:

* fixed overhead variance
* variable overhead variance

calculating overhead variances

fixed overhead variance: standard overhead *less* actual overhead

variable overhead variance: standard overhead *less* actual overhead

* An *adverse* overhead variance shows that more has been spent on overheads than the standard cost, and profit will be reduced.
* A *favourable* overhead variance shows that less has been spent on overheads than the standard cost, and profit will be increased.

It is also possible to calculate sub-variances for overhead variances, but the topic is not covered in this book. Your further studies in cost and management accounting may lead you to this topic.

conclusion

Standard costs are set in order to give individual departmental managers, responsible for aspects of the business' output, suitable targets to aim for. When actual costs are compared with standard costs, an analysis can be carried out to see why the variances and sub-variances have occurred, and to see what can be done about them for the future. Note, in particular, the way in which variances and sub-variances are calculated down to a responsibility level of an individual employee, or a small section within the business: this is the application of *responsibility accounting*.

This chapter has shown the principles of monitoring costs through variance analysis. It has explained the reasons why variances occur and has demonstrated, by means of Case Studies, how to calculate variances and sub-variances. There are other cost variances that can be calculated – for example, for overheads, and where actual production differs from standard. However, at this stage of your studies, we are more concerned with identifying the procedures for monitoring than the ability to calculate variances. It may be that your further studies of cost and management accounting will lead you to this topic again.

chapter summary

■ Standard costs are established for the main elements of cost: materials, labour and overheads.

■ Actual costs incurred are recorded.

■ A comparison is made between standard costs and actual costs, and variances are calculated.

■ Material variances are analysed between the sub-variances of:
  • price variance: (standard price – actual price) x actual quantity
  • usage variance: (standard quantity – actual quantity) x standard price

■ Labour variances are analysed between the sub-variances of:
  • rate variance: (standard rate – actual rate) x actual hours
  • efficiency variance: (standard hours – actual hours) x standard rate

■ Overhead variances are calculated for fixed and variable overheads:
  • standard overhead – actual overhead

■ Investigation should be made in order to find out why the variances have occurred and corrective action taken.

STUDENT ACTIVITIES

9.1 The owner of a sandwich shop has calculated the standard cost of a sandwich on the following basis:
  – two pieces of bread per sandwich; 20 slices in a loaf costing 50p
  – 150 grams of filling, eg meat, salmon, cheese and salad, per sandwich at an average cost of 30p
  – butter or low fat spread sufficient for 75 sandwiches at a cost of £2.20
  – each employee to make 30 sandwiches an hour
  – employees to be paid £4.50 an hour

  • What factors do you think are likely to cause variances from the standard cost for this business?
  • How would you advise the owner of the business to monitor costs through variance analysis?

9.2 From the following information you are to prepare a standard cost report (see page 127):

product: 500 cardboard boxes, size 750 mm x 400 mm x 300 mm

standard costs:	£
materials	28
labour	36
fixed overheads	18
variable overheads	15

actual costs:	
materials	38
labour	29
fixed overheads	20
variable overheads	12

- What factors do you think may have caused the variances?
- What further analysis of the cost information would you advise?

9.3 The following standard cost report for the manufacture of 600 ornamental clay garden pots, showing sub-variances for materials and labour, has been passed to you, as the cost accountant, for further action:

	standard cost	£	*actual cost*	£	*sub-variances*	£	£	
materials	900 kilos		800 kilos		price		40	ADV
	at 75p per kilo	675	at 80p per kilo	640	usage		75	FAV
							35	FAV
labour	150 hours		140 hours		rate		70	ADV
	at £5.00 per hour	750	at £5.50 per hour	770	efficiency		50	FAV
							20	ADV
overheads								
fixed		250		260			10	ADV
variable		80		60			20	FAV
TOTAL COST		1,755		1,730			25	FAV

You are to:
- show how the sub-variances for materials and labour have been calculated
- explain how you will use the variances and sub-variances as part of the process of monitoring costs

9.4 From the following data you are to calculate:

(a) materials price variance

(b) materials usage variance

(c) materials variance

(Indicate whether each variance is *adverse* or *favourable*.)

	Standard Price	Standard Usage	Actual Price	Actual Usage
Material A	£5 per kg	10 kgs	£4 per kg	12 kgs
Material B	£20 per unit	12 units	£22 per unit	10 units
Material C	£10 per litre	6 litres	£9 per litre	5 litres
Material D	£2 per metre	3 metres	£3 per metre	2.5 metres

9.5 From the following data you are to calculate:

(a) labour rate variance

(b) labour efficiency variance

(c) labour variance

(Indicate whether each variance is *adverse* or *favourable*.)

	Standard Hours	Standard Wage Rate	Actual Hours	Actual Wage Rate
Product 1	8	£5.00	7	£5.50
Product 2	3	£4.50	4	£5.00
Product 3	24	£6.00	30	£5.75
Product 4	12	£8.00	15	£8.50

10 Pricing decisions

introduction

In the previous three chapters we have considered how businesses use cost accounting techniques to calculate the cost of output – either making a product or providing a service. In this chapter we look at how the selling price to the customer is worked out. This can be quite a complex process but, at its most simple, there are two techniques used:

- ***cost-plus,*** *ie cost price, plus profit (often as a percentage of cost price) equals selling price*
- ***market led,*** *ie the selling price is determined largely by what other suppliers of similar products or services are charging*

It should be remembered that, if the business is to make a profit, then selling price must, overall, be higher than total costs. However, there are circumstances when it is possible to sell output at below the absorption cost and still increase profits – we shall investigate the pricing of 'special orders' using marginal cost pricing later in this chapter.

cost-plus pricing

The basic calculation for cost-plus pricing is: *cost price + profit = selling price*

Cost is usually calculated on the basis of absorption cost (see page 110) – which absorbs all costs into each cost unit – or standard cost (see page 116). A variation is to use marginal cost (see page 111) and, later in this chapter, we will see how marginal cost can be used to price 'special orders'.

Profit can be calculated
- *either* as a percentage mark-up on cost price (ie the profit, being a percentage of cost price, is added to cost price to give selling price)
- *or* to give a percentage return on capital employed (ie the money invested in the business)

The Case Study which follows illustrates the ways in which a company can use cost-plus pricing to determine the selling price for its products.

CASE STUDY: LEATHERCRAFT LIMITED

situation

Leathercraft Limited makes high-quality 'executive' chairs. Each year, at its factory in Mereford, it makes 2,000 chairs and its costs are as follows:

annual costs for producing 2,000 chairs

	£
Direct materials (£100 per chair)	200,000
Direct labour (£70 per chair)	140,000
PRIME COST	340,000
Overheads (fixed)	100,000
TOTAL COST	440,000

The company is currently reviewing its selling prices and is considering cost-plus pricing based on:

*   *either* a 40 per cent mark-up on cost price (ie profit is 40 per cent of cost price, which is added to cost price to give selling price)
*   *or* a 20 per cent return on capital employed

Leathercraft Limited has capital employed of £1,000,000.

solution – using cost-plus pricing

percentage mark-up method

selling price is calculated as:	£
total costs	440,000
40 per cent mark-up (40% x £440,000)	176,000
selling price	616,000

Using percentage mark-up, the selling price per chair will be:

£616,000 ÷ 2,000 chairs = £308 per chair

percentage return on capital employed method

Return on capital employed is a performance measure, expressed as a percentage, which compares profit with the capital needed to run the business (see Chapter 1, page 7). It is expressed as:

$$\frac{profit}{capital\ employed} \quad x \quad \frac{100}{1} \quad = \quad percentage\ return\ on\ capital\ employed$$

For Leathercraft Limited the capital employed is £1,000,000. A 20 per cent return on capital employed is the target return set by the company. Thus, the profit required is:

£1,000,000	x	20%	= £200,000
capital employed	x	*percentage return*	= *profit*

Selling price is calculated as:

	£
total costs	440,000
20 per cent return on capital employed (see above)	200,000
selling price	640,000

Using percentage return on capital employed, the selling price per chair will be: £640,000 ÷ 2,000 chairs = £320 per chair.

conclusion

The two methods of cost-plus pricing used in the case study give different selling prices per cost unit:

* percentage mark-up: £308 per chair
* percentage return on capital employed: £320 per chair

Whilst both methods meet the target requirements of mark-up and return on capital employed, it does not follow that Leathercraft Limited will be able to sell its chairs at either price. It might be that its customers will find a supplier who is able to produce chairs of the same quality but at a cheaper price; in other words, the price Leathercraft will charge is *market led*.

market led pricing

When a business has a product or service for which there is considerable demand and over which it has sole rights, it may be able to set and maintain its own price level (subject to government intervention on the grounds of monopoly pricing). Most businesses, however, must set their prices in comparison with other suppliers of the same or similar products and services. In the economy of the free market, buyers will tend to buy from the supplier than can produce the product, or supply the service, at least cost. Thus, in an ideal world (but not always in reality), inefficient suppliers will be forced out of the market and, in order to re-establish themselves, will have to look carefully at their costings and/or production techniques.

There are many examples of market led pricing, some of which (but not all) benefit the buyer:

* *The price of similar products*
  Supermarket shelves, as an example, often contain 'rival' brands of the same product, eg tins of baked beans, cans of cola drink. Whilst each manufacturer will always tell you that their product is infinitely superior to that of their rivals, market led pricing means that there is little, if any, difference in price. Whilst supermarket 'own brand' products are usually cheaper, the pricing is still market led, ie a similar amount less than the price of branded goods.

- *The price of seasonal products, such as fresh fruit*
  By and large the market leads the price, eg a supplier of strawberries cannot charge significantly more than the competitors.

- *The price of cars*
  It is often said that the price of cars in the UK is higher than in the rest of Europe. If a particular market is able to bear a higher price, suppliers will seek to maintain that price.

- *The price of computers*
  The price of computer hardware and software in both the UK and Europe is always much higher than the US dollar equivalent prices. Whilst many computer products are manufactured in the USA, even allowing for shipping costs, it almost seems as though Europe is regarded as a high cost (and high profit) market.

marginal cost pricing

In the long term, every business which seeks to make profits, must cover its costs and make a profit from the selling prices of its output. As we have seen earlier in the chapter, traditionally this involves cost-plus pricing techniques which add a percentage to absorption cost. However, it is common to use marginal cost when pricing 'special orders'. (Remember that marginal cost is the cost of producing one extra unit – often marginal cost is the same as prime cost.) The principle here is that, provided a business is already profitable at its current level of output, it can make additional sales at a selling price above marginal cost, but below absorption cost, and so increase its profits. The proviso is that the additional sales must be spare capacity within, for example, the factory: if, in order to sell 100 extra units, a new factory has to be bought with a capacity of one million units, then it seems unlikely that the additional sales will prove to be profitable! The key to increasing the profit from additional sales is to ensure that a contribution to profit is made from the special order: the Case Study (below) illustrates this principle.

CASE STUDY: WYVERN BIKE CO LTD

situation

The Wyvern Bike Co Ltd produces 100 bikes a week, and sells them for £100 each. Its costs are as follows:

weekly costs for producing 100 bikes

	£
Direct materials (£20 per bike)	2,000
Direct labour (£25 per bike)	2,500
PRIME COST	4,500
Overheads (fixed)	3,500
TOTAL COST	8,000

The management of the company has been approached by a mail order warehouse which wishes to buy:

- *either* 50 bikes each week at a price of £60
- *or* 100 bikes each week at a price of £40

The bikes can be produced in addition to existing production, with no increase in overheads. The special order is not expected to affect the company's existing sales. How would you advise the management?

solution

The *absorption cost* of producing one bike is £80 (£8,000 ÷ 100 bikes). The mail order warehouse is offering either £60 or £40 per bike. On the face of it, with an absorption cost of £80, both orders should be rejected. However, as there will be no increase in overheads, we can use the *marginal costing* system to help with decision making.

The *marginal cost* per bike is £45 (direct materials £20, plus direct labour £25 per bike), and so any contribution, ie selling price less marginal cost, will be profit:

- **50 bikes at £60 each**
  Although below absorption cost, the offer price of £60 is above the marginal cost of £45 and increases profit by the amount of the £15 extra contribution, ie (£60 – £45) x 50 bikes = £750 extra profit.

- **100 bikes at £40 each**
  This offer price is below absorption cost of £80 and marginal cost of £45; therefore there will be a fall in profit if this order is undertaken of (£40 – £45) x 100 bikes = £500 reduced profit.

weekly profit statements	Existing production	Existing production + 50 units @ £60 each	Existing production + 100 units @ £40 each
	£	£	£
Sales revenue (per week):			
100 bikes at £100 each	10,000	10,000	10,000
50 bikes at £60 each	–	3,000	–
100 bikes at £40 each	–	–	4,000
	10,000	13,000	14,000
Less production costs:			
Direct materials (£20 per unit)	2,000	3,000	4,000
Direct labour (£25 per unit)	2,500	3,750	5,000
Overheads (fixed)	3,500	3,500	3,500
PROFIT	2,000	2,750	1,500

The conclusion is that the first special order from the mail order warehouse should be undertaken, and the second declined. The general rule is that, once the overheads have been recovered, provided additional units can be sold at a price above marginal cost, then profits will increase.

limiting factors

Limiting factors – some aspect of the business which prevents further expansion – have been discussed earlier in the book (see Chapter 3, page 38).

Where a business sells more than one product, under normal circumstances it will be best to switch production to the product that gives the highest contribution in relation to sales. For example, a company makes two products for which the selling prices and contributions are:

	product X	product Y
selling price	£100	£200
contribution	£40	£60

With no limiting factors, the company should concentrate on making and selling product X. The reason for this is that the contribution in relation to sales is £40 on £100, ie 40 per cent when compared with product Y, where it is £60 on £200, ie 30 per cent.

Where there is a limiting factor, for example the availability of skilled labour, a business will switch production to the product which gives the highest contribution from each unit of the limiting factor (eg contribution per direct labour hour). The Case Study which follows illustrates this.

CASE STUDY: SOUND SYSTEMS LTD – LIMITING FACTORS

situation

Sound Systems Limited makes reproduction radios to 1930s' designs (but with 1990s' sound quality!). Two models are made – the 'Windsor' and the 'Buckingham'. Both products require skilled direct labour which cannot be increased in the short-term. Demand for the company's products is increasing rapidly and, while the company is taking steps to train new employees, the production manager is unsure of the 'mix' of products she should produce each week.

The information available is:

	Windsor	Buckingham
selling price per unit	£50	£100
contribution per unit	£20	£30
direct labour hours per unit	2	2

- the number of direct labour hours each week is 240.
- the weekly fixed overheads of the business are £2,000
- all of the company's output can be sold

Give the production manager your recommendations for next week's production, supporting your views with a forecast profit statement.

solution

Ignoring, for the moment, the limiting factor of direct labour, the better model for the company to produce is the Windsor, because this gives a higher contribution in relation to sales:

- Windsor: £20 contribution on £50 of sales = 40 per cent
- Buckingham: £30 contribution on £100 of sales = 30 per cent

However, as direct labour is the limiting factor, the company should maximise the contribution from each hour of direct labour:

- Windsor: contribution per direct labour hour £20 ÷ 2 hours = £10
- Buckingham: contribution per direct labour hour £30 ÷ 2 hours = £15

Therefore, the company should utilise fully its direct labour hours in production of the Buckingham, ie 120 units will be made (240 hours ÷ 2 hours per unit).

The forecast weekly profit statement will be as follows:

forecast weekly profit statement

	£
Sales of Buckingham (120 units x £100)	12,000
Contribution (120 units x £30)	3,600
Less overheads (fixed)	2,000
Profit	1,600

Note however that, by taking this action, no Windsor models will be produced – the marketing director will not be too keen on this as it may be difficult to re-establish the Windsor in the market when production of this model can be restarted following the completion of training for new employees. In practice, it is likely that both models will be made, but with preference being given to the Buckingham.

fixed and variable costs

In making pricing decisions it is also important to consider the balance between fixed costs and variable costs. For example, it is often possible to carry out a production process in one of two different ways: the first might be labour intensive, requiring only a few inexpensive machines; the second might need costly machines, but few operators. Thus, with the first method, variable costs are high, but fixed costs are low; with the second method, variable costs are low, but fixed costs are high. The method that is chosen will depend on the costs involved, the likely demand and selling price of the product, and the availability of finance. We shall be looking at these topics in more detail in the next chapter.

chapter summary

- *Cost-plus pricing* is calculated as:
  cost price + profit = selling price

- In cost-plus pricing, profit can be calculated
  - *either* as a percentage mark-up on cost price
  - *or* to give a percentage return on capital employed

- *Market led pricing* occurs where there are other suppliers of the same or similar products and services, and their pricing structure has to be followed.

- *Marginal cost pricing* is where a product is sold at a price which is above marginal cost, but below absorption cost. It is used for pricing 'special orders' which utilise spare capacity.

- Limiting factors are an aspect of the business which prevents further expansion. To maximise profits, the company must produce the product which gives the highest contribution from each unit of the limiting factor.

STUDENT ACTIVITIES

10.1 Wyvern Private Hospital Limited carries out a large number of minor operations for day patients. For next year it plans 2,500 operations based on the following costs:

annual costs for 2,500 minor operations

	£
Direct materials (£200 per operation)	250,000
Direct labour (£400 per operation)	500,000
PRIME COST	750,000
Overheads (fixed)	200,000
TOTAL COST	950,000

The hospital is reviewing its pricing policy for minor operations and is considering cost-plus pricing based on:

- either a 25 per cent mark-up on cost price
- or a 20 per cent return on capital employed

The capital employed for the minor operations section of the hospital is £1,000,000.

You are to calculate the cost per minor operation using the two cost-plus pricing methods.

10.2 Investigate the selling prices of the following products:

- a large white sliced loaf of bread
- a can of cola drink
- a litre of unleaded petrol
- a standard sized tin of baked beans
- a kilo of fruit or vegetables (depending on the season)

Find out:

- the selling price of each of the products from two outlets of a similar size, eg two large supermarkets, two corner shops, two large garages, two market stalls.
- a comparison of the price of similar products sold at the same outlet, eg rival brands of cola drinks (for petrol, find two garages close to each other – preferably selling different brands – and compare the prices for the different grades of petrol)

What conclusions do you draw about market led pricing?

10.3 The Last Company is famous for its 'Snowdon' range of hill-walking boots. The management of the company is considering the production for next year and has asked you, as cost clerk, to help with certain financial decisions.

The following information is available:

Wholesale selling price (per pair)	£60
Direct materials (per pair)	£20
Direct labour (per pair)	£18
Overheads (fixed)	£200,000 per year

The company is planning to manufacture 12,500 pairs of boots next year.

(a) You are asked to calculate:
- the absorption cost per pair
- the marginal cost per pair
- the profit or loss if 12,500 pairs of boots are sold

(b) A mail order company, Salesbypost Limited, has approached The Last Company with a view to selling the 'Snowdon' boot through its catalogue. Salesbypost Ltd offers two contracts:
- *either* 2,500 pairs of boots at £45 per pair
- *or* 5,000 pairs of boots at £37 per pair

As The Last Company usually sells through specialist shops, it is not expected that 'normal' sales will be affected. These 'special orders' are within the capacity of the factory, and overheads will remain unchanged. You are to advise the management as to whether this offer should be accepted; illustrate your answer with profit statements.

10.4 Dean Limited makes two products – A and B. Both products use direct materials which are currently in short supply. At present the company can obtain only 500 kilos of the direct materials each week. The production manager seeks your guidance as to the 'mix' of products she should produce each week. The information available is:

	A	B
selling price per unit	£150	£200
contribution per unit	£30	£50
kilos of direct materials per unit	2	4

- The weekly fixed overheads of the business are £4,000.

You are to give the production manager your recommendations for next week's production, supporting your views with a forecast profit statement.

Nice 'n Tasty and Wyvern Engineering – costing and pricing

for BTEC Element 11.3
Identify approaches used in business to monitor the use of financial resources

INTRODUCTION

This Evidence Collection Exercise looks at the ways in which two different types of business use costing systems to monitor financial resources:

- for business 1 – a takeaway sandwich bar – you will be gathering costs, taking pricing decisions, and demonstrating the use of absorption costing and marginal costing.
- for business 2 – an engineering company – you will be showing how a standard costing system can be used as part of the monitoring process, and how an activity based costing system could be introduced.

BUSINESS 1: NICE 'N TASTY

A friend of yours, Jo Smythe, is planning to set up a business selling takeaway sandwiches. She is calling her business 'Nice 'n Tasty' and has seen a suitable empty shop unit in a shopping arcade just off the main street in your town. The unit is quite small, but the rent and rates are reasonable at £200 per week. Jo plans to promote her business on the basis of freshly-made sandwiches, and a range of tasty fillings. She will work in the business herself, and will employ an assistant for five hours each day (six days a week) at a pay rate of £4.50 an hour.

Jo asks you to help with the costing and pricing aspects of her business, and provides you with a list of cost items:

- bread
- butter or healthy spread
- sandwich fillings
- packaging
- assistant's wages (see above)
- electricity
- telephone
- water
- rent and rates (see above)

TASKS FOR BUSINESS 1 _____

1. Write a report to Jo indicating whether the above costs are
   - fixed
   - variable
   - semi-variable

   Explain to her why it is important to distinguish between them.

2. Calculate the approximate weekly costs for the business. To help with this, Jo tells you that she expects to sell 1,200 packs every week, each containing a round of sandwiches (ie two pieces of bread). The fillings – meat, salmon, cheese and salad – will cost approximately 30p per sandwich. As far as the other costs are concerned, you may make reasonable assumptions provided that you are able to justify them.

3. Once all the costs are known (or estimated), you are to calculate the cost price of each pack of sandwiches, using absorption costing. You then recommend to Jo that she should use cost-plus pricing with a mark-up of 30 per cent (ie cost price of sandwiches, plus 30 per cent). As all packs will be sold at a standard price, Jo asks you to suggest the selling price (which you can round up to 5p above), and to ensure that this price is in line with – and perhaps slightly cheaper than – that charged by other shops in town. If you consider that a market led price is more appropriate, you should justify it.

4. Prepare a sample profit statement for a typical week, based on the costs and selling price decided in tasks 2 and 3. The profit statement will show the profit available for drawings by Jo.

5. A local factory has asked Jo to supply the canteen with 60 packs of sandwiches on each of the five working days in a week. Jo considers that she and her assistant will be able to cope with this extra work and is keen to take it on. It is unlikely that her normal sales will be affected by this order, as the factory employees do not have time to get into town during their lunch break. The factory canteen manager asks for a 35 per cent discount off the normal selling price of the sandwiches.

   Using the marginal costing system, explain to Jo whether or not she should take on this order. Whatever your advice to her, you are to prepare a profit statement for a typical week, incorporating this order.

BUSINESS 2: WYVERN (ENGINEERING) LIMITED

You are the cost accountant of Wyvern (Engineering) Limited. The company makes engine castings for the car industry.

You have recently calculated a standard cost for a new engine casting that is to be made from next week at the rate of 100 per week. The job will pass through two departments of the company: the foundry (where the metal will be cast), and the machine shop (where the castings will be machined to the customer's specifications).

The standard cost (for 100 castings) is as follows:

> **100 castings**
>
> **Materials**
>   60 kg of ordinary steel at £4.00 per kg
>   25 kg of high-tensile steel at £12.50 per kg
> **Labour**
>   20 hours foundry-workers' wages at £13.00 per hour
>   25 hours in the machine shop at £14.00 per hour
> **Overheads**
>   fixed £450
>   variable £125

When the 100 castings are completed, at the end of the week, it is found that actual results are:

- **Materials**
    65 kg of ordinary steel at £3.80 per kg
    24 kg of high-tensile steel at £13.00 per kg
- **Labour**
    22 hours foundry-workers' wages at £12.50 per hour
    23 hours in the machine shop at £14.25 per hour
- **Overheads**
    fixed £440
    variable £135

TASKS FOR BUSINESS 2

1. Prepare a standard cost report for the week showing the total cost variance and other cost variances, indicating whether they are favourable or adverse.

2. Explain how the cost variances can be used by management for monitoring costs.

3. At present the company uses labour hours as the basis by which overheads are charged to each department (ie the foundry and the machine shop). You know that £300 of the fixed overheads relates to inspection costs; the inspection requirements are:
    - foundry – one casting in 50 to be inspected
    - machine shop – one casting in 10 to be inspected

    Each inspection, whether in the foundry or the machine shop, takes the same length of time and is carried out by the same inspector.

    You are to suggest and explain (with the use of cost data) a more appropriate method of charging inspection costs to each department.

Section

4

decision making

11 Break-even analysis

introduction

This chapter looks at the relationship between fixed costs and variable costs: the nature of these costs has been examined already in Chapter 7. We shall now study the relationship between them in break-even analysis, which is the point at which a business makes neither a profit nor a loss.

In this chapter we look at:
- *the nature of fixed and variable costs*
- *break-even point*
- *break-even analysis, by calculation, by table, by graph*
- *interpretation of break-even*
- *limitations of break-even analysis*
- *margin of safety, ie the amount by which sales exceed the break-even point*
- *use of break-even analysis*

fixed and variable costs

In Chapter 7 we have seen that the main elements of total cost for most manufacturing businesses comprise:
- materials
- labour
- overheads

We know that, by nature, costs are:
- fixed, or
- variable, or
- semi-variable

In brief, fixed costs remain constant over a range of output levels, despite other changes. Variable costs vary directly with changes in output levels. Semi-variable costs combine both a fixed and variable element, eg the telephone bill comprises the fixed rental for the line, together with the variable element of call charges.

Do remember that the nature of costs can change as the business changes. For example, a fixed cost, such as factory rent, is only likely to be fixed at or near current production levels: if output is doubled or trebled, then it is likely that an additional factory will need to be rented. In this way, the fixed cost is no longer fixed!

For the purposes of break-even analysis we need to distinguish between fixed and variable costs, and be able to pick out from semi-variable costs the amounts of the fixed and variable elements.

break-even point

Break-even is the point at which neither a profit nor a loss is made.

In order to use break-even analysis, we need to know:

- selling price (per unit)
- production costs
    - variable costs (such as materials, labour) per unit
    - overhead costs, and whether these are fixed or variable
- limitations, such as maximum production capacity, maximum sales

CASE STUDY: FLUFFY TOYS LIMITED – BREAK-EVEN

situation

Fluffy Toys Limited manufactures soft toys, and is able to sell all that can be produced. The variable costs (materials and direct labour) for producing each toy are £10 and the selling price is £20 each. The fixed costs of running the business are £5,000 per month. How many toys need to be produced and sold each month for the business to cover its costs, ie to break-even?

solution

This problem can be solved by calculation, by constructing a table, or by means of a graph. Which method is used depends on the purpose for which the information is required:

- the *calculation method* is quick to use and is convenient for seeing the effect of different cost structures on break-even point
- the *table method* shows the amounts of fixed and variable costs, sales revenue, and profit at different levels of production
- the *graph method* is used for making presentations – for example, to the directors of a company – because it shows in a visual form the relationship between costs and sales revenue, and the amount of profit or loss at different levels of production

Often the calculation or table methods are used before drawing a graph. By doing this, the break-even point is known and suitable scales can be selected for the axes of the graph in order to give a good visual presentation.

calculation method

Selling price per unit	£20
Less variable costs per unit	£10
Contribution per unit	£10

Each toy sold gives a contribution (selling price, less variable costs) of £10. This contributes towards the fixed costs and, in order to break-even, the business must have sufficient £10 'lots' to meet the fixed costs. Thus, with fixed costs of £5,000 per month, this business must sell £5,000 ÷ £10 = 500 toys each month. The break-even formula is:

$$\frac{total\ fixed\ costs\ (£)}{contribution\ per\ unit\ (£)} = break\text{-}even\ point\ (number\ of\ units)$$

table method

units of production	fixed costs	variable costs	total cost	sales revenue	profit/(loss)
	£	£	£	£	£
100	5,000	1,000	6,000	2,000	(4,000)
200	5,000	2,000	7,000	4,000	(3,000)
300	5,000	3,000	8,000	6,000	(2 000)
400	5,000	4,000	9,000	8,000	(1,000)
500	5,000	5,000	10,000	10,000	nil
600	5,000	6,000	11,000	12,000	1,000
700	5,000	7,000	12,000	14,000	2,000

graph method

A graphical presentation uses money amounts as the common denominator between fixed costs, variable costs, and sales revenue. The graph appears at the top of the next page.

notes to the graph

- With a break-even graph, it is usual for the vertical axis (the 'y' axis) to show money amounts; the horizontal axis ('x') shows units of production/sales.
- The fixed costs are unchanged at all levels of production, in this case they are £5,000.
- The variable costs commence, on the 'y' axis, *from the fixed costs amount,* not from 'zero'. This is because the cost of producing zero units is the fixed costs.
- The fixed costs *and* the variable costs form a *total costs line.*
- The point at which the total costs and sales revenue lines cross is the break-even point.
- From the graph we can read off the break-even point both in terms of units of production, 500 units on the 'x' axis, and in sales *value,* £10,000 on the 'y' axis.

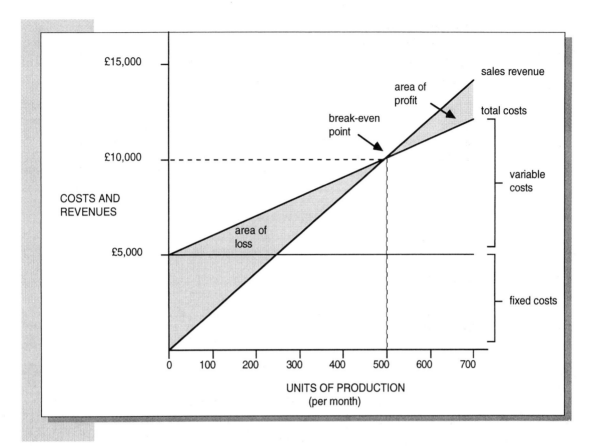

hints for drawing a break-even graph

- In an accountant's break-even chart *all lines are straight.* This means that only two points need be plotted for each line; for example, with sales, choose a number that is fairly near to the maximum expected, multiply by selling price per unit, and this is the point to be marked on the graph. As the sales line always passes through zero, you now have two points along which to draw a straight line.

- When drawing a break-even graph it is often difficult to know what total value to show on each axis, ie how many units, and/or how much in costs and revenues? As a guide, look for a maximum production or sales level that will not be exceeded: this will give the 'x' axis. Multiply the maximum sales, if known, by the unit selling price to give the maximum sales revenue for the 'y' axis. If the figure for maximum sales is not known, it is recommended that the break-even point is calculated before drawing the graph so that the extent of the graph can be established.

- A common error is to start the variable costs from the zero point instead of the fixed costs line.

interpretation of break-even

In interpretation of break-even, it is all too easy to concentrate solely on the break-even point. However, the graph tells us much more than this: it also shows the profit or loss at any level of production/sales contained within the graph. To find this, simply measure the gap between sales revenue and total costs at a chosen number of units, and read the money amounts off on the 'y' axis (above break-even point it is a profit; below, it is a loss). From the graph in the Case Study above, read off the profit or loss at:

1. 700 units,   2. 650 units,   3. 200 units,   4. 400 units (answers below).

Break-even analysis, whether by calculation, by table, or by graph, is not used solely by a manufacturer: all organisations can use the concept. For example, a shop will wish to know the sales it has to make each week to meet costs; a sports centre will wish to know the ticket sales that have to be made to meet costs; a youth club might wish to know how many raffle tickets it needs to sell to meet the costs of prizes and of printing tickets.

Once the break-even point for an organisation has been reached, the *additional* contributions form the profit. For example, if the business considered above was selling 700 toys each month, it would have a total contribution of 700 x £10 = £7,000; of this the first £5,000 will be used to meet fixed costs, and the remaining £2,000 represents the profit (we can also read this off from the break-even graph in the Case Study). This can be shown by means of a financial statement as follows:

MONTHLY PROFIT STATEMENT

	£
Sales (700 toys at £20 each)	14,000
Less variable costs (700 toys at £10 each)	7,000
Contribution (to fixed costs and profit)	7,000
Less monthly fixed costs	5,000
Profit for month	2,000

limitations of break-even analysis

The problem of break-even analysis is that it assumes that the relationship between sales revenue, variable costs and fixed costs, remains the same at all levels of production. This is a rather simplistic view because, for example, in order to increase sales, a business will often need to offer bulk discounts, so reducing the sales revenue per unit at higher levels. The limitations of break-even analysis can be summarised as follows:

- The assumption is made that all production is sold. There is no point in preparing the cost data, calculating the break-even point, and estimating the profits to be made if the product will not sell in sufficient quantities. However, break-even analysis is useful for a new business in order to establish the level of sales that must be achieved to reach break-even point. The feasibility of reaching that level of sales must then be considered by the owners of the business.

- All costs and revenues are expressed in terms of straight lines. However, this is relationship is not always so. As indicated above selling prices may vary at different quantities sold; in a similar way, variable costs alter at different levels as a business takes advantage of lower prices to be gained from bulk buying, and/or more efficient production methods.

- Fixed costs do not remain fixed at all levels of production: for example, a decision to double production is likely to increase the fixed costs – an increase in factory rent, for example. Fixed costs are often described as 'stepped costs', because they increase by a large amount all at once and, when plotted on a graph, they take the form of a step:

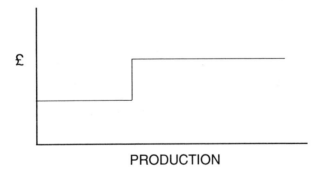

PRODUCTION

- It is not possible to *extrapolate* the graph or calculation; by extrapolation is meant extending the lines on the graph beyond the limits of the activity on which the graph is based. For example, in the Case Study just considered, the graph cannot be extended to, say, 1,000 units of production and the profit read off at this point. The relationship between sales revenues and costs will be different at much higher levels of production.

- The profit or loss shown by the graph or calculations is probably only true for figures close to current production levels – the further away from current figures, the less accurate will be the profit or loss shown.

- A further disadvantage of break-even analysis is that it concentrates too much attention on the break-even point. While this aspect is important to a business, other considerations such as ensuring that production is as efficient as possible, and that costs are kept under review, are just as important.

break-even: margin of safety

The margin of safety is the amount by which sales exceed the break-even point. It can be expressed either as a number of units or as a percentage, using the following formula:

$$\frac{current\ production - break\text{-}even\ production}{current\ production} \times \frac{100}{1} = percentage\ margin\ of\ safety$$

In the Case Study earlier in this chapter, if current production is 700 units, while the break-even point is 500 units, the margin of safety is 200 units or, expressed as a percentage:

$$\frac{700 - 500}{700} = 29\ per\ cent\ margin\ of\ safety$$

In interpreting margin of safety, we can say that production (and sales) can fall by 200 units or 29 per cent before the business reaches break-even point and ceases to make a profit.

contribution to sales ratio

The contribution to sales (or C/S) ratio expresses, as a percentage, the amount of contribution in relation to the amount of the selling price:

$$\frac{contribution\ (£)}{selling\ price\ (£)} \times \frac{100}{1} = contribution\ to\ sales\ ratio$$

The ratio can be calculated on the basis of a single unit of production or for the whole business.

We have already touched on the contribution to sales ratio in the previous chapter (see page 142). In break-even analysis, if fixed costs are known, we can use the C/S ratio to find the sales value at which the business breaks-even, or the sales value to give a target amount of profit.

example

Referring back to the Case Study (Fluffy Toys Limited), the C/S ratio (on a per unit basis) is:

$$\frac{contribution\ (£)}{selling\ price\ (£)} \times \frac{£10^*}{£20} \times \frac{100}{1} = 50\ per\ cent$$

* selling price (£20), minus variable costs (£10), equals contribution £10

Fixed costs are £5,000 per month (see page 151), so the sales value to break-even is:

$$\frac{fixed\ costs\ (£)}{C/S\ ratio\ (£)} \times \frac{100}{1} = \frac{£5,000}{50\ (see\ above)} \times \frac{100}{1} = £10,000$$

If the directors of Fluffy Toys Limited wish to know the sales that must be made to achieve a target profit of £2,000 per month, the C/S ratio is used as follows:

$$\frac{(\textit{fixed costs + target profit})}{\textit{C/S ratio \%}} \quad x \quad \frac{\textit{100}}{\textit{1}} \quad = \quad \textit{required level of sales}$$

$$\frac{(£5,000 + £2,000)}{50} \quad x \quad \frac{100}{1} \quad = \quad £14,000$$

when to use break-even analysis

Break-even analysis is often used:

before starting a new business
The calculation of break-even point is important in order to see the level of sales that the new business needs in order to cover costs, or make a particular level of profit. The feasibility of achieving the level can then be considered by the owner of the business, and other parties such as the bank manager. Break-even analysis will be included in the business plan.

when making changes to a business
The costs of a major change in a business will need to be considered by the owners and/or managers. For example, a large increase in production will, most likely, affect the balance between fixed and variable costs. Break-even analysis will be used as part of the planning process to ensure that the business remains profitable.

to measure profits and losses
Within the limitations of break-even analysis (see page 154), profits and losses can be estimated at different levels of output from current production. (Remember that this can be done only where the new production is close to current levels and where there is no major change to the structure of costs – ie it is not possible to extrapolate.)

to answer 'what if?' questions
Questions such as 'what if sales fall by 10 per cent?' and 'what if fixed costs increase by £1,000?' can be answered – in part at least – by break-even analysis. The effect on the profitability of the business can be seen, subject to the limitations noted earlier. A question such as 'what if sales increase by 300 per cent' can only be answered by examining the effect on the nature of the fixed and variable costs and then re-calculating the break-even point.

to evaluate alternative viewpoints
There are often different ways of making a product; this is particularly true of a manufacturing business. For example, a product could be made:
- either, by using a labour-intensive process, with a large number of employees supported by basic machinery
- or, by using expensive machinery in an automated process with very few employees.

In the first case, the cost structure will be high variable costs (ie labour) and low fixed costs (ie depreciation of machinery). In the second case, there will be low variable costs and high fixed costs. Break-even analysis can be used to examine the relationship between the costs which are likely to show a low break-even point in the first case, and a high break-even point in the second. In this way, the management of the business is guided by break-even analysis; management will also need to know the likely sales figures, and the availability of money with which to buy the machinery.

chapter summary

- In break-even analysis it is essential to distinguish between fixed costs and variable costs.

- The relationship between sales revenue, and fixed costs and variable costs can be used to show, by means of a calculation, a table, or by means of a graph, the break-even point.

- Break-even is the point at which neither a profit nor a loss is made.

- The break-even calculation is:

  $$\frac{total\ fixed\ costs\ (\pounds)}{contribution\ per\ unit\ (\pounds)} = break\text{-}even\ point\ (number\ of\ units)$$

- Break-even analysis can show:
  - break-even point in units of production
  - break-even point in value of sales
  - profit or loss at a given level of production/sales

- The limitations of break-even analysis are that:
  - the assumption is made that all production is sold
  - costs and revenues are expressed in straight lines
  - fixed costs do not remain fixed at all levels of production
  - it is not possible to extrapolate the break-even graph or calculation
  - the profit or loss is probably only true for figures close to current production levels
  - it concentrates too much on break-even point

- Margin of safety is the amount by which sales exceed the break-even point.

- Break-even analysis is often used:
  - before starting a new busines
  - when making changes to a business
  - to measure profits or losses
  - to answer 'what if?' questions
  - to evaluate alternative viewpoints

STUDENT ACTIVITIES

11.1   Cuddly Toys Limited manufactures a popular children's teddy bear. At present production is limited by the capacity of the factory to 50 bears each week. The following information is available:

selling price per teddy bear	£20
direct materials per teddy bear	£4
direct labour per teddy bear	£5
weekly fixed costs:	
• factory rent and rates	£100
• fuel and power	£20
• other costs	£34

You are to find the weekly break-even point by constructing a table and drawing a graph. Check your answer by calculation.

11.2   D Bradman, a manufacturer of cricket bats, has the following monthly costs:

material cost	£ 8 per bat
labour cost	£12 per bat
selling price	£35 per bat
overheads	£12,000

You are to:
• Draw up a table showing costs, sales revenue, and profit or loss for production of bats in multiples of 100 up to 1,200.
• Draw a graph showing the break-even point.
• Prove your answer by calculation.
• Read off the graph the profit or loss if (a) 200 bats, and (b) 1,200 bats are sold each month: prove the answer by calculation.
• If production is currently 1,000 bats per month, what is the margin of safety, expressed in units and as a percentage?

11.3   Bert Peters is the owner of a petrol filling station which has the following weekly costs:

Cost of petrol from oil company	50p per litre
Selling price	55p per litre
Overheads (fixed cost)	£750

You are the accountant of the business and are asked to:

- Draw up a table showing costs, sales revenue, and profit or loss for sale of petrol in multiples of 1,000 litres up to 20,000 litres.
- Draw a graph showing the break-even point.
- Prove your answer by calculation.
- Read off the graph the profit or loss if (a) 12,000 litres, and (b) 18,000 litres are sold each week: prove the answer by calculation.
- If sales are currently 18,000 litres each week, what is the margin of safety, expressed in litres and as a percentage?

11.4 Peter Parkinson is a central heating engineer who has designed a special type of thermostatic valve for use in heating systems. He has decided to set up in business to manufacture the product and he has carried out market research which suggests that demand for the product will be between 9,000 units and 20,000 units per annum. Accordingly he has produced the following estimated costs at different levels of production:

budgeted sales (number of units)	9,000	12,000	15,000	20,000
direct materials (£)	27,000	36,000	45,000	60,000
direct labour (£)	9,000	12,000	15,000	20,000
production overheads (£)	48,000	54,000	60,000	70,000
administration, selling and distribution expenses (£)	18,000	18,000	18,000	18,000

Each thermostatic valve will sell for £10.

Peter asks you to help him interpret the results, and in particular he wishes to know:
(a) the profit or loss he will make at each level of production
(b) the break-even point
(c) the fixed amount of production overheads

One market-research survey suggested that a level of sales of 25,000 units per annum might be achieved. Peter asks you to rework the budget at this level of production and to calculate the net profit or loss which will be achieved. He asks you to let him know of any limitations to the usefulness of your figures at this level.

12 Make or buy decisions

introduction

Sometimes a manufacturing business is faced with the decision of whether to make a product itself or to buy in the completed item from a supplier. In a service business a similar decision often has to be made whether to provide a service 'in-house' or to buy it in from a supplier.

In this chapter we will look at:
- *what is a make or buy decision?*
- *financial aspects, including the effect on fixed and variable costs, the use of marginal costing, and the opportunity cost*
- *other aspects of make or buy decisions*
  - *quality of work from outside suppliers, and reliability of supplies*
  - *advantages and disadvantages of buying in*
- *types of make or buy decisions*

what is a make or buy decision?

A make or buy decision is a management decision whether to make a product (or supply a service) 'in-house', or to buy in the product (or service) from an outside supplier.

Examples of make or buy decisions include:
- a car manufacturer needing many different components to make the car – some components will be manufactured in-house while others will be bought from outside suppliers
- a local authority facing the decision whether to provide a refuse collection service itself, or to buy in the service from an outside contractor

Make or buy decisions offer alternative ways for a business to increase output:

- ***expanding its own production facilities***
  Here the business will acquire extra factory (and possibly office) space, buy new machinery, employ more staff.

- ***buying in from outside suppliers***
  The business buys in completed components or parts which can then go straight into the product as it is being assembled. By buying in components, some part of the existing production facility will be freed up, so enabling it to be switched to other work, eg assembly of the product using the bought in components.

Note that a business with declining sales will have to consider the opposite of these two ways, ie reducing its own production facilities, or cancelling contracts to buy in from outside suppliers.

Whilst there are a number of considerations before taking a make or buy decision, the cost involved in the decision and the effect on profit – both financial aspects – are usually uppermost in the mind of management. We shall look firstly at the financial aspects, and then at the other aspects.

financial aspects of make or buy decisions

the effect on fixed and variable costs

Make or buy decisions affect the cost structure of the business, particularly the relationship between fixed and variable costs. For example, a business seeking to increase output (as we have just seen) can:

- *either* expand its own production facilities, which will mainly affect its fixed costs (ie rent of factory, depreciation of new machinery), with a smaller effect on variable costs

- *or* buy in from outside suppliers, which will mainly affect its variable costs (ie bought in components are classed as direct materials), with a smaller effect on fixed costs

As you will appreciate, the first course of action takes a long-term view and assumes that the increase in production can be sustained for a number of years. The second course of action is rather more flexible (ie the number of components bought in can be varied to meet demand) and could be either a long-term arrangement, or for the short-term with, perhaps, the possibility of expanding own production facilities in the future.

the use of marginal costing

When considering make or buy decisions, comparisons need to be made between:

- the marginal cost of making the product in-house

  and

- the price quoted by the outside supplier

The one with the lower price is, in financial terms, the better choice; however there may well be non-financial aspects to consider (see page 166).

Note that:

– marginal cost is the cost of producing extra output, and generally comprises the variable costs, plus any specific costs such as special machinery needed to make the product

– fixed costs shared amongst functions of the business are not considered because they will continue to be incurred by the business

– the opportunity cost (see below) should also be considered for make or buy decisions

opportunity cost

Opportunity cost is the profit that is foregone when a particular course of action is taken.

In make or buy decisions we must consider the resources used (eg factory space, machines) when goods are made in-house. The use of these resources may cause other work to be lost or curtailed. The loss of contribution from this other work needs to be added to the marginal cost in order to make the decision (see Case Study below). The make or buy decision can be expressed now as a comparison between:

• the marginal cost of making the product in-house, plus the contribution from lost or curtailed work

   and

• the price quoted by the outside supplier

The lower price is the better choice in financial terms.

CASE STUDY; WYVERN ALARMS LMITED

situation
Wyvern Alarms Limited manufactures high quality security alarms called 'Wyvern Super'. These are sold to alarm companies who instal and maintain them.

Until now, Wyvern Alarms has prided itself on its in-house production line – raw materials are bought in, and all manufacturing and assembly is carried out at its factory in Wyvern. With the rise in crime rates, the company is finding that demand for its products is increasing. It has designed a cheaper alarm called 'Wyvern Value'.

The point has been reached when decisions must be taken about buying in components and sub-assemblies from outside suppliers.

The cost accountant of Wyvern Alarms, Sheila Smythe, has obtained prices from potential suppliers for two components detailed below.

control boxes

These comprise a metal box with a hinged, lockable cover. The box is spray painted in white, with the company logo applied by means of a transfer. It is not considered that quality will be compromised if this item is bought in from an outside supplier.

These are the two alternatives:

1 The cost of making each control box in-house at the current level of 5,000 units each year is:

	£
direct materials	2.50
direct labour	5.50
variable overheads	1.50
fixed overheads	5.50
total cost	15.00

There is no other use for the specialist production machinery required to make this product.

2 An outside supplier has quoted a price of £10 per unit (based on Wyvern's requirements of 5,000 units each year).

processor controllers

At the heart of each 'Wyvern Super' security alarm is a control unit operated by microprocessors. Assembly of these units from raw materials is a complex and time-consuming task: a quality supplier who is able to offer guaranteed control units has been identified.

These are the two alternatives:

1 The cost of making each processor controller in-house at the current level of 5,000 units each year is:

	£
direct materials	15.00
direct labour	20.00
variable overheads	10.00
fixed overheads	20.00
total cost	65.00

If the product is bought in from a supplier, the production facilities released can be used to assemble 1,000 'Wyvern Value' alarms (which do not use a processor controller) each year with a selling price of £300 per unit and variable costs of £200 per unit.

2 An outside supplier has quoted a price of £50 per controller (based on Wyvern's requirements of 5,000 units each year).

Should Sheila Smythe 'make' or 'buy' ?

solution

CONTROL BOXES
The marginal cost of producing each control box is:

	£
direct materials	2.50
direct labour	5.50
variable overheads	1.50
marginal cost	9.50

Although the supplier's price of £10 per unit is below absorption (total) cost of £15, it is 50p above the marginal cost of in-house manufacture.

As there is no other use for the production machinery currently being used, the decision should be to continue making this component in-house.

PROCESSOR CONTROLLERS
The marginal cost of producing each processor controller is:

	£
direct materials	15.00
direct labour	20.00
variable overheads	10.00
marginal cost	45.00

The supplier's price of £50 per unit is below absorption cost of £65, but is £5 above the marginal cost of in-house manufacture.

However, the production facilities released can be used to make 1,000 'Wyvern Value' alarms each year. The comparison is therefore:

in-house manufacture

		£
marginal cost of manufacture		
5,000 units at £45	=	225,000
plus contribution which will be lost from 'Wyvern Value' alarms:		
1,000 units at £300 – £200	=	100,000
		325,000

buying in cost from outside supplier

		£
5,000 units at £50	=	250,000

Therefore, by buying processor controllers the company has the potential to increase profits by £325,000 – £250,000 = **£75,000**

other aspects of make or buy decisions

As well as financial data, there are a number of other aspects that must be taken into account with make or buy decisions.

buying in – aspects of the supplier

Aspects of the supplier that will need to be considered include:

* *quality*

  Will the goods and services be of an acceptable quality? Will that quality be maintained over a period of time?

* *reliability*

  Is reliability of deliveries assured? (Many manufacturing companies – eg car manufacturers – receive components on a 'just-in-time' [JIT] basis, ie the components are delivered straight to the production line, and are assumed to be of the specified quality.) Will the supplier continue to trade for the foreseeable future? (Bankruptcy of a major supplier will have serious repercussions for the buying in company.)

* *price*

  Will the price of bought in goods and services remain relatively constant? Has the supplier quoted a keen price in order to get the business and will then increase the price for further supplies? Has a keen price been quoted because there is a recession on and the supplier needs the business? (If so, the supplier may raise prices and/or may be less willing to do business once the recovery is under way.) Are the goods being bought from abroad? (If so, the price quoted by the supplier is likely to be in a foreign currency – this leaves the buying company open to increased prices because of exchange rate fluctuations.)

* *confidentiality*

  Will the supplier respect the confidential nature of designs and recipes, etc?

* *legal requirements and other standards*

  Will the supplier be able to adapt to legal requirements and, for example, European Union safety standards, both now and in the future?

advantages of buying in

* *flexibility*

  Items can be bought in as and when needed and, while the supplier will require a contract to supply set quantities, it is rather easier to increase or decrease the current order than to open or close in-house production facilities.

* *the need for specialist equipment*

  Where a production process requires specialist equipment to make the component, it is often advantageous to obtain the components from an outside supplier. This is better than buying the equipment for in-house use and then having it standing idle, because there is insufficient volume of business to utilise it fully.

- *finance*

  By buying in, there is no need for major capital expenditure on new production facilities. This will be an important consideration when finance is 'tight'.

- *management time*

  When considering a make or buy decision, the amount of management time required is likely to be considerably greater in running an in-house production process than in arranging to buy in goods from an outside supplier. (Nevertheless, management time will need to be spent in ensuring that the supplier provides goods and services of the right quality.)

- *avoidance of high fixed costs*

  When products are bought in, the often high fixed costs (and high break-even point) of making a product in-house can be avoided. This is especially relevant when there are uncertainties as to future demand for the finished product – caused, for example, by changes in fashion or by possible economic recession. This aspect is illustrated in the Case Study on the next page.

- *maximising contribution through limiting factors*

  We have already seen how limiting factors can have a restrictive effect on the output of a business (page 142 of Chapter 10). A company should use its own production facilities to maximise the contribution from each unit of the limiting factor. Other production, with a lower contribution per unit of the limiting factor, should be considered for buying in from an outside supplier.

- *reduced training costs*

  With bought in products and services there can be a reduction in the costs of training employees, when compared with in-house production. The difference in these costs becomes more marked where skills, for example engineering, are needed to make the product.

- *reduced lead time*

  Setting up an in-house production line takes time – the decision is taken, a factory is bought, equipment installed, staff recruited and trained, materials purchased. All-in-all, there is a long lead time from making the decision through to seeing completed components made in-house. By contrast, the lead time from an established supplier can be quite short – specifications are agreed, contracts are signed, and the supplier can commence production. Where the components are needed quickly, buying in may offer the only solution.

disadvantages of buying in

These disadvantages relate mainly to the quality of the bought in product and have been highlighted earlier. Alongside this is the feeling that bought in goods and services are 'outside our control' – although this can be overcome by taking steps to ensure that both the bought in and in-house products are virtually indistinguishable.

CASE STUDY: THE EFFECT OF FIXED COSTS

situation

Severn Computers Limited and Avon Computers Limited are computer manufacturers. Their products sell widely throughout the UK and the other countries of the European Union.

Severn Computers makes its computers entirely in-house from individual components. By contrast, Avon Computers buys in completed computers built to its specifications by a supplier in Taiwan.

The profit statements for the two companies for last year are as follows:

	Severn Computers	Avon Computers
	£000	£000
Sales	5,000	5,000
Less variable costs	1,500	3,000
Contribution	3,500	2,000
Less fixed costs	3,000	1,500
Profit	500	500

Unfortunately, recession is affecting the European Union and sales of computers are down by 20 per cent. What will be the effect of this on the two companies?

solution

With sales down by 20 per cent to £4,000,000, there will be a similar fall in variable costs. By contrast, fixed costs remain unchanged. Their profit statements are likely to be as follows:

	Severn Computers	Avon Computers
	£000	£000
Sales (reduced by 20%)	4,000	4,000
Less variable costs (reduced by 20%)	1,200	2,400
Contribution	2,800	1,600
Less fixed costs (unchanged)	3,000	1,500
Profit/(loss)	(200)	100

As you can see, the company with the high fixed costs (Severn Computers) is more vulnerable to a downturn in sales: it has a higher break-even point and a lower margin of safety (see Chapter 11). However, the company with lower fixed costs (Avon Computers) is still able to show a profit. The conclusion to be drawn is that, if to make a product in-house requires a large increase in fixed costs, the company leaves itself vulnerable to a downturn in sales; by buying in, the effect of the downturn is reduced. (It must be said, however, that if sales had increased by 20 per cent, then the profits of Severn would have been higher than those of Avon, thus showing the advantages of high fixed costs/low variable costs in a rising market.)

types of make or buy decisions

In this chapter we have looked in some depth at make or buy decisions which involve the buying in of components used in a manufactured product. Reference has also been made to the buying in of services – for example, a local authority which buys in a refuse collection service from an outside contractor.

Recent years have seen a rapid increase in the use of bought in (or 'contracted out' or 'outsourced') services – particularly so by local authorities, central government, and hospitals. These organisations engage in Compulsory Competitive Tendering (CCT) for many of their services; under CCT, services are offered for tender to private businesses. Examples of bought in services are common: Group 4 Security transporting remand prisoners to court, refuse collection by contractors, buffet service on trains provided by private businesses.

In a school or college, the provision of a minibus is a type of make or buy decision – should a minibus be bought by the school or college, or should it be hired from the local bus company when a trip is planned? (see Evidence Collection Exercise 4). In a business, make or buy decisions can be extended to services such as payroll, catering, security, vehicle maintenance – each of these being provided by an outside contractor.

As we have seen, all make or buy decisions combine:

* financial aspects
* other aspects, such as quality and reliability

The cheapest solution in financial terms may well not prove to be the best buy, and the make or buy decision must be taken in the overall context of the effect on the company.

---

chapter summary

- Make or buy decisions are concerned with whether to make a product (or supply a service) in-house, or to buy in the product (or service) from an outside supplier.

- In a make or buy decision, consideration must be given to financial and other aspects.

- In *financial* terms the costs to compare are:
  * the marginal cost of making the product in-house, plus the contribution from lost or curtailed work
    and
  * the price quoted by the outside supplier
  The lower price is the better choice in financial terms.

- *Other, non-financial, aspects* cover principally the quality and reliability of outside contractors. The change to the business overall must be considered, particularly the effect of changes in fixed and variable costs.

- Where there is a limiting factor, a company will seek to use its own production facilities to maximise the contribution from each unit of the limiting factor, and buy in other products and services.

STUDENT ACTIVITIES

12.1 (a) Sesame Shoes Limited manufactures shoes at its factory in Wyvern. A company in the Far East has offered to manufacture one particular style of shoe – the 'Paris' design – at a cost of £20 per pair.

The cost accountant of Sesame Shoes has prepared the following cost statement (per pair of shoes) – based on current production levels – for the 'Paris' design.

	£
direct materials	10.00
direct labour	5.00
variable overheads	3.00
fixed overheads	5.00
total cost	23.00

Note: there is currently no other use for the factory space and production machinery used to make the 'Paris' design.

Advise the management of Sesame Shoes whether or not, in financial terms, the shoes should be bought in from the Far Eastern manufacturer.

(b) Apart from financial data, what other aspects should the management of Sesame Shoes consider before making a final decision?

12.2 Pentland Pumps Limited manufactures electric pumping equipment used in industry and agriculture. At present all parts are made in-house from raw materials. The company is considering buying in pump motors from an outside supplier in order to release facilities for a new product, an 'olde worlde' handpump for decorative (and practical) use.

The following information is available:
- the cost of making each pump motor in-house at the current level of production of 3,500 pumps per year is:

	£
direct materials	40.00
direct labour	25.00
variable overheads	20.00
fixed overheads	15.00
total cost	100.00

- an outside supplier has quoted a price of £95 per motor

- if pump motors are bought in from an outside supplier, the company will be able to make 750 'olde worlde' handpumps each year, with a selling price of £250 per unit and variable costs of £150 per unit

You are to advise the management of Pentland Pumps Limited whether or not, in financial terms, the motors should be bought in from the outside supplier.

12.3 Wyvern Micros Limited manufactures computers at its factory in Wyvern. It sells to retailers in Britain and the other countries in the European Union. At present the computers are built in-house from raw materials. The profit statement for last year is as follows:

		£000
Sales		2,500
less:	variable costs	750
	fixed costs	1,500
Profit		250

A new managing director has recently been appointed. She plans to scale down the British manufacturing operations and to buy in completed computers built to the company's specifications by a supplier in the Far East. Working with the management accountant she has re-worked last year's profit statement to show the effect on costs, as follows:

		£000
Sales		2,500
less:	variable costs	1,500
	fixed costs	750
Profit		250

Although the profit is the same she argues that, with an imminent economic recovery in Europe, the company will be better placed to take advantage of an increased demand for computers. She talks of a forecast increase in sales of 30 per cent. The finance director is more pessimistic about the prospects of recovery and suggests that the company should be prepared for a fall in sales of 30 per cent.

You are to:

(a) Prepare budgeted profit statements for next year based on:
   – the managing director's assertion that sales will increase by 30 per cent
   – the finance director's view that sales will fall by 30 per cent

(b) Write a note explaining the reasons for changes in the profits.

13 Capital investment appraisal

introduction

In this chapter we look at the methods used to help with decision making about capital investment projects – for example, if we need a new photocopier, shall we buy a Toshiba or a Canon model? The methods of capital investment appraisal are:

- *payback*
- *accounting rate of return*
- *discounted cash flow*

In this chapter we explain what capital investment appraisal involves, and then look at each of the three methods by means of a Case Study, and make a comparison between them. At the end of the chapter, we look at a further capital investment appraisal method called internal rate of return.

what is capital investment appraisal?

You will already know from your studies that all resources are limited in supply. As a result there is a need to use resources in such a way as to obtain the maximum benefits from them. To do this it is necessary to choose between various alternatives available; for example, on a personal level, we have to make decisions such as:

Should I save my spare cash in a bank or in a building society?

Should I save up for a car, or should I buy on hire purchase?

Which make of car, within my price range, should I buy?

Should I rent a house or should I buy, taking out a mortgage?

While these decisions are personal choices, the management of businesses of all sizes is constantly faced with making choices, as are local authorities and central government.

The management of any business is constantly having to make decisions on *what* to produce, *where* to produce, *how* to produce, and *how much* to produce. Similar considerations must be the concern of businesses which provide services. For each major choice to be made, some method of appraisal has to be applied to ensure that, whatever decisions are taken, they are the right ones. This means that it is necessary to look at all the alternatives available and to choose the one that is going to give the most benefit to the business. For example, a business may have to decide whether to replace its existing machinery with new, more up-to-date machinery. If it decides on new machinery, it then has to choose between different makes of machine and different models, each having a different cost and each capable of affecting output in a different way. At the same time a decision has to be made whether to pay cash outright, to buy on hire purchase, or to lease.

The objective of capital investment appraisal is to enable a business to decide whether or not to invest in a particular capital investment project and, where there are a number of viable alternatives, to decide in which of them to invest.

what is a capital investment project?

A capital investment project is the spending of money now in order to receive benefits (or reduce costs) in future years. It is illustrated below in fig 13.1:

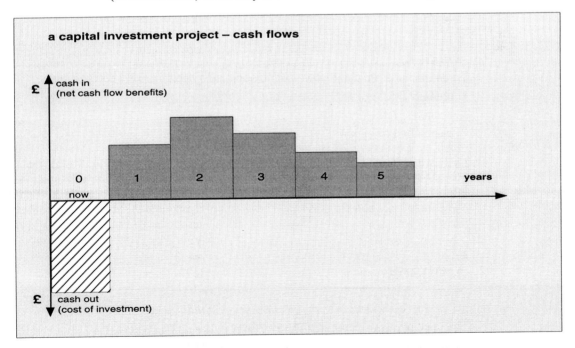

Fig. 13.1 *A capital investment project – cash flows in and out*

Here the capital expenditure now (often stated as 'year 0') brings benefits (or reduced costs) in future years. The business needs to apply capital investment appraisal methods to ensure that the investment decision is the correct choice.

CASE STUDY: A NEW MACHINE

situation

A business needs a new machine and has to make the choice between Machine Y and Machine Z. The initial cost and the net cash flow over five years (income, less running expenses but *not* depreciation) to the business have been calculated for each machine as follows:

	MACHINE Y	MACHINE Z
Initial cost	£20,000	£28,000
Net cash flow:		
Year 1	£8,000	£10,000
Year 2	£12,000	£10,000
Year 3	£5,000	£8,000
Year 4	£4,000	£9,000
Year 5	£2,000	£9,000

Only one machine is needed and, at the end of five years, the machine will have no value and will be scrapped. To finance the project, the business can borrow money at 10 per cent per annum. Which machine should be chosen?

solution

Three methods are commonly used to appraise a capital project such as this:

- payback
- accounting rate of return
- discounted cash flow

Each of these methods will be considered in this chapter in order to help the business to make its decision. At the end of the chapter we will also look at how the internal rate of return (or discounted cash flow yield) is used in order to make a direct comparison between projects which have different amounts of capital investment at the start.

payback

This method, as its name implies, sees how long it takes for the initial outlay to be repaid by the net cash flow coming in. Thus Machine Y costs £20,000 and it is expected that the net cash flow over the first two years will equal the cost. The payback time for Machine Y is, therefore, two years, while that for Machine Z is three years. So, using payback, Machine Y is preferable. The faster the payback the better, particularly where high technology or fashion projects are concerned – they may be out-of-date before they reach the end of their useful lives. Earlier cash flows are likely to prove more accurate estimates than later cash flows. Thus, if two projects have the same payback, the one with the earlier cash flows is preferred. For example:

	A	B
Year 1	£8,000	£12,000
Year 2	£12,000	£8,000

While both projects, A and B, have the same payback period of two years, B is the preferred project under the payback method.

advantages of payback

- it is easy to calculate
- it is easy to understand
- it places emphasis on the earlier cash flows, which are more likely to be accurate than later cash flows
- an ideal capital investment appraisal method for high technology projects

disadvantages of payback

- all cash flows after the payback period are ignored
- within the payback period it fails to take into account the timing of net cash flows, eg Machine Y would still have had a payback of two years even if the cash flows for years one and two had been reversed (as noted above, earlier cash flows are to be preferred)

accounting rate of return

The accounting rate of return method is used to calculate the percentage rate of return to the business from a project, based on the initial cost of the project, as follows:

$$\frac{(Total\ estimated\ cash\ flow* - Initial\ cost)}{Estimated\ life\ of\ project} \quad \times \quad \frac{100}{Initial\ cost}$$

* Scrap value or residual value, if any, at the end of the project would be taken into account.

The preferred project will be the one that has the highest percentage accounting rate of return.

For Machine Y, the accounting rate of return is calculated as follows:

$$\frac{(£31,000 - £20,000)}{5\ years} \quad \times \quad \frac{100}{£20,000} \ = \ 11\ per\ cent$$

For Machine Z, using the same formula, the accounting rate of return is 12.9 per cent; so, using this method, Machine Z is slightly preferable.

advantages of accounting rate of return

- it is relatively easy to calculate
- all cash flows are used
- it is easy to understand the results

disadvantage of accounting rate of return

The timing of cash flows is completely ignored, ie the same result would have been reached if the cash flows for Machine Y had been £1,000, £1,000, £1,000, £1,000 for each of the first four years, and £27,000 in year five (as noted under payback, earlier cash flows are to be preferred)

discounted cash flow

Discounted cash flow (DCF) is a capital investment appraisal method which recognises that money has a time value. For example, supposing that today a friend asks you to lend her £1 and offers to repay you either tomorrow, or in one year's time, which will you choose? The answer is clear: you would want the money back sooner rather than later because, if you don't intend to spend it, you can always save it in a bank or building society, where it will earn interest. Thus, as you will probably know from your studies, the rate of interest represents the time value of money.

Using £1 as an example, if it is invested with a bank or building society at an interest rate of 10 per cent per year, it will increase as follows:

original investment	£1.00
interest at 10% on £1	£0.10
value at end of first year	£1.10
interest at 10% on £1.10	£0.11
value at end of second year	£1.21

As you will appreciate this is the technique of compound interest, with which you may already be familiar. So, with interest rates of 10 per cent per year, we can say that the future value of £1 will be £1.10 at the end of year one, £1.21 at the end of year two, and so on; thus £1 set aside now will gain in value so that, at some time in the future, we will have access to a larger sum of money. However, supposing that we were to receive £1 at the end of year one, what is it worth to us now? To find the answer to this, we need to carry out the following calculation:

$$£1 \times \frac{100}{110^*} = £0.91$$

* 100 per cent, plus the rate of interest (in this example, 10 per cent).

Therefore, if we had £0.91 now and invested it at 10 per cent per year, we would have £1 at the end of year one. We can say that the *present value* of £1 receivable in one year's time is £0.91. In the same way, £1 receivable in two years' time is £0.83, calculated as follows:

$$£1 \times \frac{100}{110} \times \frac{100}{110} = £0.83$$

We can build up a *table of factors* (for 10 per cent interest rate) as shown in fig 13.2 (below):

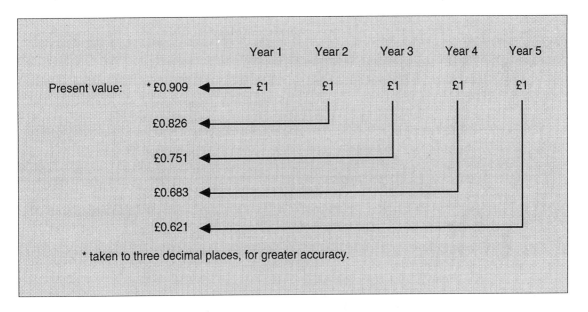

Fig. 13.2 Table of present value factors for 10 per cent interest rate

Using your calculator, check that the table of factors above is correct. Put '1' into your calculator and multiply by 100 ÷ 110 for the first year; multiply the result by 100 ÷ 110 for the second year; and so on. As you are doing this, do not forget the basic principle that *money has a time value* and, from this, the further into the future that we expect to receive money, then the lower is its *present value*.

Let us now return to the problem of the business which has to choose between Machine Y and Machine Z. We will look at this assuming, firstly, a rate of interest or *cost of capital* of 10 per cent. (Cost of capital is the rate of return that a business expects on its money, or the rate of interest it has to pay when borrowing money.) For each machine, the expected net cash flows are multiplied by the relevant factor to give the *discounted cash flow*; the difference between total discounted cash flow and the initial cost is the *net present value* of the project.

For Machine Y the calculations are:

	Cash Flow £		Discount Factor		Discounted Cash Flow £
Year 0*					(20,000)
Year 1	8,000	X	0.909	=	7,272
Year 2	12,000	X	0.826	=	9,912
Year 3	5,000	X	0.751	=	3,755
Year 4	4,000	X	0.683	=	2,732
Year 5	2,000	X	0.621	=	1,242
			Net Present Value (NPV) =		4,913

* Year 0 is the commencement of the project when the initial costs are paid.

Note that the initial cost is shown in brackets because it is a cost, whereas the net cash flows are positive amounts; net present value is the sum of all cash flows.

For Machine Z the figures are:

	Cash Flow £		Discount Factor		Discounted Cash Flow £
Year 0					(28,000)
Year 1	10,000	X	0.909 =		9,090
Year 2	10,000	X	0.826 =		8,260
Year 3	8,000	X	0.751 =		6,008
Year 4	9,000	X	0.683 =		6,147
Year 5	9,000	X	0.621 =		5,589
			Net Present Value (NPV) =		7,094

Here, with a cost of capital of 10 per cent, Machine Z is better, producing a considerably higher net present value than Y. Note that both machines give a positive net present value at 10 per cent: this means that either machine will be of benefit to the organisation but Machine Z is preferable; a negative NPV would indicate that a project should not go ahead.

Thus, using a discounted cash flow method, future cash flows are brought to their value now; this means that, the further on in time that cash flows are receivable, the lower is the net present value. As this is often a difficult concept to grasp, to put it another way, future cash flows are all brought back to a common denominator which is *now*.

advantages of discounted cash flow

- all cash flows are used
- the timing of cash flows is taken into account
- using a table of factors the calculations are easy to make

disadvantages of discounted cash flow:

- the cost of capital rate is, in practice, difficult to ascertain
- the meaning of net present value is not always clear to users of the information
- the project with the higher net present value does not, in pure financial terms, always represent the better project

capital investment appraisal: comparison

It is unlikely that a business will rely on one method only; instead two or more criteria might be required before a capital project is given the go-ahead. Supposing, for example, that the business, having to choose between Machines Y and Z, applied the following criteria: "projects must have a payback period not exceeding two and a half years, and must have a positive net present value at a 10 per cent cost of capital." How do the two machines compare?

	MACHINE Y	MACHINE Z
Payback	2 years	3 years
NPV at 10 per cent	£4,913	£7,094

Under the criteria that the business has laid down, Machine Y would be chosen. However, Machine Z seems a better project on the net present value basis and is only rejected because it does not meet the payback requirement; also Machine Z has the better accounting rate of return (at 12.9 per cent, instead of 11 per cent for Machine Y). However, the capital expenditure required for Machine Z is £8,000 greater than Machine Y – something which NPV does not take fully into account. To obtain a better analysis, we need to use the method of *internal rate of return*.

internal rate of return

The principles of discounted cash flow can be developed further in order to calculate the capital investment appraisal method of internal rate of return (IRR) – this method is also known as DCF yield. Note that internal rate of return is different from accounting rate of return.

The internal rate of return is the interest rate at which net present value exactly balances the initial investment. In other words, it shows the interest rate (or cost of capital) at which the investment 'breaks-even', ie income equals expenditure, but still applying DCF principles.

To calculate IRR we start with a cost of capital which gives a positive net present value – for example, 10 per cent cost of capital for Machine Y gives a NPV of £4,913. We increase the cost of capital by one or two percentage points each time until, eventually, it becomes negative. For example:

MACHINE Y

Cost of Capital	Present Value of Cash Flow £	Capital Investment £	Net Present Value £
10%	24,913	(20,000)	4,913
12%	23,946	(20,000)	3,946
14%	23,025	(20,000)	3,025
16%	22,177	(20,000)	2,177
18%	21,987	(20,000)	1,987
20%	20,619	(20,000)	619
22%	19,915	(20,000)	(85)
24%	19,242	(20,000)	(758)

The net present value that balances the present value of cash flow with the initial investment lies between 20% and 22% – closer to 22% than 20%, so we can call it approximately 22% (an answer to the nearest one or two percentage points is acceptable for most decisions).

Internal rate of return can also be found by means of a graph (see fig 13.3 on the next page) and just two calculations.

The procedure is:
- select a low cost of capital percentage which gives a positive net present value figure
- select a high cost of capital percentage which gives a negative net present value figure
- prepare a graph with
  - on the 'y' axis net present values (both positive and negative) for the range of the two calculations
  - on the 'x' axis cost of capital for the percentages used in the two calculations
- plot the positive and negative figures for net present values against their respective cost of capital percentages
- join the two points in a straight line (as it is a straight line graph there is no need to calculate more than one positive and one negative net present value)
- read off the internal rate of return from the 'x' axis

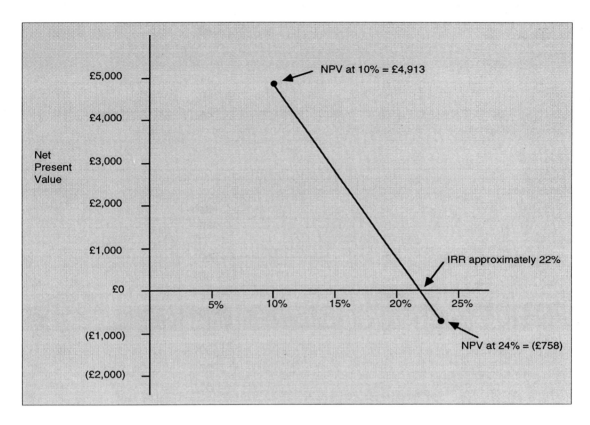

Fig. 13.3 Internal rate of return graph

Returning to our two machines, Y and Z, the IRR for Machine Z is approximately 20%. Thus, Machine Y gives a higher IRR and is, thus, the preferred capital investment. The reason for this is that Machine Y requires a lower capital expenditure, and the timing of the cash flows is weighted towards the earlier years.

The decision criteria when using IRR is to:
- accept the higher IRR, where there is a choice between different capital investments
- accept projects with an IRR greater than the cost of borrowing (the cost of capital).

Thus, while IRR can be compared between two (or more) different capital investments, it can also be applied to cost of capital. In the example we have followed in this chapter, the cost of capital is 10%. The organisation could have gone ahead with either investment. However, if the cost of capital had been 20%, Machine Z would have been rejected and Machine Y accepted (with an approximate 2% margin above cost of capital).

■ Capital investment appraisal uses a number of methods to help in management decision making.

■ The methods include payback, accounting rate of return and discounted cash flow.

■ Businesses often use a combination of two or more appraisal methods before making decisions about major projects.

■ Internal rate of return (also known as DCF yield) is used to rank projects, still applying the principles of discounted cash flow.

STUDENT ACTIVITIES

TABLE OF DISCOUNTED CASH FLOW FACTORS

Cost of capital	*10%*	*12%*	*14%*	*16%*	*18%*	*20%*	*22%*	*24%*
Year 1	0.909	0.893	0.877	0.862	0.847	0.833	0.820	0.806
Year 2	0.826	0.797	0.769	0.743	0.718	0.694	0.672	0.650
Year 3	0.751	0.712	0.675	0.641	0.609	0.579	0.551	0.524
Year 4	0.683	0.636	0.592	0.552	0.516	0.482	0.451	0.423
Year 5	0.621	0.567	0.519	0.476	0.437	0.402	0.370	0.341
Year 6	0.564	0.507	0.456	0.410	0.370	0.335	0.303	0.275

13.1 Using the discounted cash flow method, rework the calculations for Machines Y and Z, in the chapter, using the factors for (a) 14 per cent, and (b) 20 per cent per annum from the table above.

13.2 Robert Smith is considering two major capital investment projects for his engineering business. Only one project can be chosen and the following information is available:

	Project A	**Project B**
	£	£
Initial capital outlay	80,000	100,000
Net cash inflows, year: 1	40,000	20,000
2	40,000	30,000
3	20,000	50,000
4	10,000	50,000
5	10,000	49,500

The initial capital outlay will occur immediately and you may assume that the net cash inflows will arise at the end of each year. Smith's estimated cost of capital over the five year period is 12 per cent per annum.

To assist Robert Smith make his decision you, as his accountant, are asked to:

* Produce numerical assessments of the two projects based on the following capital investment appraisal methods:

  (a) payback

  (b) net present value (NPV)

  (c) accounting rate of return

* Comment on the relative merits of the project appraisal methods, and advise Robert Smith which capital investment, if either, should be undertaken. Present your advice in the form of a letter to your client, enclosing the calculations you have made for above. His address is Unit 27, Factory Estate, Newtown, Wyvern County, WV2 1ER.

13.3 Ken Shah needs some printing equipment for his publishing firm. He has to choose between the following methods of acquisition:

* purchase of the equipment for cash
* purchase under a hire purchase contract, involving an initial deposit and two annual payments
* hire of the equipment

The following information is available:

cash price of equipment	£10,000
period of use in Shah's firm	5 years
scrap value at end of use	£1,000
initial deposit under hire purchase contract	£4,000
Two annual hire purchase payments due at end of first year and end of second year	£4,000 each
Hire of equipment, five annual hire charge payments due at end of each year	£2,500 each

Shah's estimated cost of capital over the five year period is 10 per cent per annum.

You are his Finance Director and to assist Ken Shah make his decision, you are asked to:

* produce numerical assessments of the three methods of acquisition using discounted cash flow methods
* advise Ken Shah, in the form of a memorandum, of the best method of acquisition

13.4 Calculate the internal rate of return (DCF yield) to the nearest two per cent for projects A and B in question 13.2. Prove your answer by means of a graph.

Comment on the IRR for both projects.

EVIDENCE
COLLECTION
EXERCISE

The minibus – decision making in organisations

for BTEC Element 11.4
Investigate how organisations use financial information to assess
performance and make decisions

INTRODUCTION

This Evidence Collection Exercise requires you to gather information and obtain costs for a capital investment project. You will present your findings in the form of a briefing paper for a meeting at which the decision to approve or not approve the project is to be made. In particular, you will need to show in the briefing paper:

- how you have gathered the information
- the decision making techniques (eg break-even, capital investment appraisal) you have used
- how you have analysed the data in order to make appropriate recommendations
- how you have justified the recommendations

THE MINIBUS PROJECT

Most schools, colleges and youth centres make use of a minibus. Depending on demand (and the availability of capital) this is either bought, or hired as required. However, it is rare for a full financial appraisal to be made of what is, after all, a major capital investment project.

In this Exercise you are to investigate the provision of a minibus for your school, college, or youth centre. The various ways of providing the minibus are set out in the diagram on the next page.

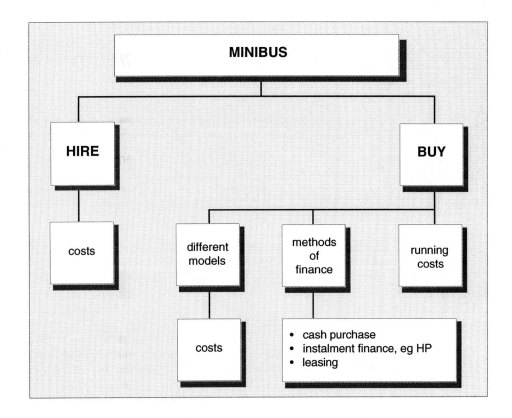

notes _____

- If the minibus is hired, basic insurance will be included in the hire charge, but there may be a cost for additional insurance.

- If the minibus is bought, there will be costs for insurance, road fund licence, membership of a recovery organisation (such as the AA or RAC) and servicing. With a new vehicle it is often possible to purchase an extended warranty for an additional two or three years beyond the manufacturer's warranty: this should reduce the incidence of unexpected repair costs.

- When comparing 'hire' or 'buy' there is no need to consider the cost of fuel (petrol or diesel), nor – if the driver is to be paid – the cost of the driver's wages. The reason for this is that the cost of these items will be the same whether the minibus is hired or bought.

- As far as possible, compare like with like, ie the same make of minibus for both 'hire' and 'buy'.

TASKS

1. Research the costs involved in 'hire' or 'buy':
    *   It is suggested that, for hire charges, you work on the basic unit of a one-day hire charge (there may well be savings for longer hire periods – you can find these out).
    *   If the minibus is purchased, it is suggested that you estimate the annual cost based on running costs (excluding fuel) and depreciation. (For depreciation you can assume that the vehicle will be kept for five years before trade-in; the value at trade-in can be assessed by using vehicle price guides which are commercially available.)

2. From the costs calculated in task 1, you can assume that:
    *   the hire charges per day are a variable cost
    *   the annual cost (if the minibus is bought) is fixed

    Use break-even analysis to plot on a graph the point at which the cost of hire (in terms of the number of hire days) equals the annual fixed cost of the purchased vehicle. The graph is likely to take the following form:

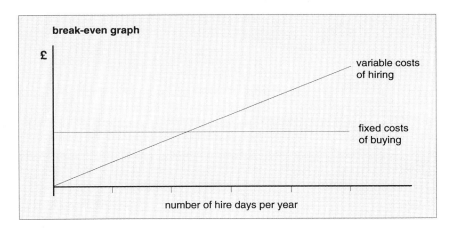

    Write up your conclusion in terms of "if usage is above a certain number of hire days it is better to buy; if below, it is better to hire." You can also make reference to cheaper hire charges for longer periods, such as weekends and weeks – depending on the likely usage at your school, college or youth centre.

3. For both 'hire' and 'buy', apply the capital appraisal method of discounted cash flow for five years:
    *   with 'hire', use the hire charge based on either the break-even number of hire days from task 2 or, more realistically, the most likely actual number of hire days at your school, college or youth centre
    *   with discounted cash flow
        – assume an estimated life of five years (the expected trade-in value at the end of year 5 – see task 1 – should be added back as income and multiplied by the year five factor)

- for cost of capital, use the current rate for business loans from a major bank
- do not forget to show the annual costs of insurance, servicing, etc (but exclude depreciation – because it is a 'non-cash' expense)

notes

- As both 'hire' and 'buy' are costs (rather than income), the one with the smaller cost figure of net present value is, using this method, the better.
- You might collect sufficient information to be able to apply other capital investment appraisal methods. For example, you could use payback to assess the purchase option where you know the number of days' use of the vehicle per year – the income will be the money saved from hiring set against the cost of buying.
- The figures may not work out as neatly as in the exercises – with this project we are dealing with real-life! If you make assumptions, always justify what you have done with a note.

4. Investigate different methods of buying the minibus:
   - cash purchase
   - instalment finance (eg hire purchase)
   - leasing
   Useful sources of information include newspapers, books, advertisements.

   Include in your briefing paper a summary of the advantages and disadvantages of each method. Wherever possible, make reference to up-to-date information, eg the selling price of the minibus, hire purchase amounts, leasing amounts – where there are different timescales (such as a three or five year hire purchase contract), make reference to this. Look out for special offers – such as cheap finance on vehicles – which should be mentioned in your briefing paper.

5. Prepare your briefing paper, ensuring that it provides evidence of
   - gathering information
   - use of decision making techniques
   - analysis of data
   - justification of your recommendation
   Do mention other aspects of the investment project that you consider to be relevant – the notes have been given to guide you, but their scope can be widened.

index